A
HISTORY
OF
BICYCLES

A
HISTORY
OF
BICYCLES

SERENA BEELEY

—WELLFLEET—
P R E S S

PICTURE CREDITS

The Author and Publisher would like to thank the following for their permission to reproduce the pictures in this book:–

COLOUR IMAGES: National Cycle Museum: 15, 16, 18, 22–4, 30, 31, 35–7, 42–5, 49–51, 56–8, 61, 63, 64, 66, 67, 76, 83, 84, 86, 88, 91, 100, 102–4, 107, 108, 114, 118 and 121; *The History of Transport*, published by Studio Editions Ltd., 1992: 12, 14, 60, 85 and 108; The Mary Evans Picture Library: 17, 21 and 82; Peter Newark's Historic Pictures: 33 and 40; The Victoria and Albert Museum: 54; Janssen Print, Nijmegen, Holland: 67 and 68; The Dalkeith Publishing Co.: 72; Crown copyright © H.M.S.O.: 77; Nottinghamshire County Council, Leisure Services Department: 78, 80, 98, 112, 115 (above) 116 and 117; Kunstgewerbemuseum, Zurich: 87, 89, 101, 102, 110 and 111; Nationaal Fietsmuseum Velorama: 90; BFI Stills, Posters and Designs: 115; Action-Plus Photography: 119, 120, 124, 126 and 129–140.

BLACK AND WHITE IMAGES: Stadsuitgeverij, Amsterdam, Holland: 5, 76, 113 and 142; The Hulton Picture Library: 13 and 99; *The History of Transport* published by Studio Editions Ltd, 1992: 16, 23, 25 (above), 26, 28, 30, 39 (below), 48, 59, 61–2, 65, 79, 83, 91–3, 94, 95, 100, 105, 116 and 117; The Rohauer Collection: 20; Peter Newark's Historical Pictures: 25 (below), 27 and 47 (centre); *The American Bicycler*, privately published in Boston, 1880: 9, 13, 21, 29, 32, 34, 36, 39, 41, 44, 45, 47, 56, 143 and 144; National Cycle Museum: 46; *The Boy's Modern Playmate*, published by Frederick Warne and Co., London and New York, 1891: 47 and 63; Nationaal Fietsmuseum Velorama (Holland): 55 and 56; Bedfordshire Record Office: 62 (below); *Cycling Weekly*: 106, 109, 122, 123, 126, 127 and 129; United Press International: 129; Foto H.A. Roth: 128.

Publisher's Note

The publishers have made every effort to locate and credit copyright holders of material reproduced in this book, and they apologize for any omissions.

A History of Bicycles
First published 1992 by Wellfleet Books
an imprint of Book Sales Inc.
110 Enterprise Avenue
Secaucus, New Jersey 07094

ISBN 1-55521-744-3

Printed and bound in Singapore

Contents

FOREWORD

I was about eleven when I was first introduced to cycling by my father, himself a keen, one might say devoted, cyclist who unearthed an 18 inch frame from some second hand store and built it up with 22 inch wheels. I can still remember the anguish of waiting, the machine all gleaming with fresh enamel, new saddle and shining plated wheels, for its completion. It was three or four weeks before the tyres were bought, whether because the small size, unusual in those days, or because they had to wait until my father could afford them I do not know. The cycle completed, then the teaching to ride. Up and down the street I would pedal, my father running beside holding the saddle to steady me. And the marvellous moment when I stopped to turn around and saw him some way back. I had cycled by myself!

This was the entrance to a new world. Easy access to the country, the equal joys of speed and of ambling, the cooling swoop down hill in the hot summer and the sharp frost of winter with the wonderland of tree branches silvered by frost all shining in the winter sunlight, the traffic-free lanes and one's own breath like a small cloud in front, transformed life.

In my young man's days, like nearly all Clubmen, I rode only lightweights, Claud Butler, Grubb, Selbach etc . . . In my maturer years I discovered Rudge Whitworth and the John Marston Sunbeam. I enjoyed cycling but knew nothing of how the cycles themselves had come about. The names of Drais, MacMillan and Michaux were unknown to me and even the name Dunlop was only a brand of tyre.

There was a long road between the Hobby Horse and my youthful lightweights and cycles of maturer years. Even longer between the Hobby Horse and the wonderful exotic racing machines of today as ridden in the Milk Race in Britain, in the Tour de Trump in the States and in that most famous cycle race of all time, the Tour de France. This road has been explored by Serena Beeley in her book *A History of Bicycles*. She has travelled its full length, pausing at each milestone, the MacMillan, the Michaux velocipede, the Rotary and Sociable tricycles, the Ordinary, the Crypto Bantam and the Facile, pedals and treadles, on to more recent ancestors of the end of the nineteenth century, the diamond frame and loop frames from which all modern cycles have sprung. The results of Serena Beeley's explorations, including a peep round the next bend in the road to try to catch a glimpse of the cycles of tomorrow, are in this book. Would that it had been available when I was young.

James Maynard.

INTRODUCTION

Of all the many inventions of the human mind, the bicycle is among the most universally used and valued. It represents a method of converting energy into transportation that is more efficient than any other and affords opportunities for mobility to many people all over the world who lack access to motorized vehicles, or have indeed rejected them in favour of cycling.

The history of the bicycle is a chronicle of inventiveness, experimentation and innovation. The standard model with which we are familiar today is a descendant of the Safety bicycle first produced over 100 years ago, but the original idea of producing a two-wheeled human-powered vehicle goes back to the late eighteenth century, when the "Draisienne", a saddled bar attached to two wheels, appeared on the streets of Paris. Although it was several decades before anything approaching the Safety came into existence, the story of cycling had begun.

It is possible to divide this story into two distinct periods. The first, from 1861 to 1910, was a time of experimentation in design, culminating in the establishment of the diamond frame on which most models have since been based. It was then that the practical skills of the master mechanic and wheelwright were gradually taken over by the manufacturing companies, so that through mass production what began as a rich man's toy became available to the general public.

During the second period, from 1910 to the present day, development has continued but has tended to concentrate on refining and improving the existing shape to create the luxury mounts of today. There has been a greater emphasis on accessories, on experiments with lightweight alloys and complex gearing systems, and on creating a wider range of machines to match the needs of different users: children, shoppers, commuters, tourers and racers.

Within these two broad divisions, this book covers the major innovations in design, technology and engineering, as well as the important social questions that were raised by the various stages in the bicycle's development. For as the new industry grew, cycle-riding spread to encompass many areas of people's lives. Apart from its obvious use as a cheap and convenient form of transport, the cycle and its relations, the tricycle and tandem, offered opportunities for new recreational and sporting activities. Increased numbers of cyclists on the road meant that new legislation had to be introduced to govern basic safety standards. Clubs were formed to regulate the activities of sporting riders and to safeguard the interests of cyclists in general against the encroachment of the motor car. After some opposition, women also took to the roads and with their new freedom of movement they found the strength to defy convention and demand equal rights with their male counterparts.

During the early years, one new design followed another in rapid succession as engineers introduced a series of ever more sophisticated refinements. When Pierre Michaux added cranks and pedals to the front wheel of the cumbersome Draisienne, the extremely popular Velocipede was born. However, Velocipede-mania lasted only until the demand for greater speed on lighter frames produced the elegant Ordinary, with its larger driving-wheel at the front and smaller weight-saving wheel at the rear.

The Ordinary, however, remained a mount for the young athletic male who could leap on and off its high saddle. Other would-be road-users were confined to tricycles and quadricycles. During the 1870s and 1880s, therefore, many engineers concentrated on producing commercially successful multi-wheelers and on developing Dwarf Ordinaries that could be ridden by the old, the very young, and by women who were still hampered by voluminous skirts.

In 1879 Lawson invented the rear driving geared bicycle, but it was not until the appearance of the Rover Safety in 1885 that the superiority of the rear-wheel chain-drive became really evident. At about the same time Humber replaced the short chain-stays with stays long enough to permit a straight seat tube, and the diamond-frame came into existence.

The early decades of this century marked the heyday of the bicycle. Its adoption by vast numbers of working people gave them the opportunity to explore the countryside during their leisure hours as well as a cheap method of getting to and from their places of work. Whole families took to the road, and there was a considerable increase in membership of the cycling clubs. The major sporting events created legendary heroes as records continued to be broken year by year. When motor manufacturers began to make cheaper and cheaper cars in the 1920s and 1930s, however, the bicycle lost its attractions for family use, and for many people in the Western world cycling came to be seen predominantly as an inferior alternative to owning a motorized vehicle.

Since then, interest in the bicycle has waxed and waned, although it has always maintained a devoted following of enthusiasts. There have been subtle improvements to the early Safeties, including the introduction of much lighter materials. Such technical advances have produced a revival in the use of the bicycle and a parallel revival in the cycle trade. In the decades following World War II every aspect of construction has been the subject of research and experiment, from the length, diameter and gauge of the tubing used, to the proportions of the different parts to one another. But, apart from such models as the Moultin small-

wheeler, developed in the 1960s, most bicycles have remained true to the same fundamental shape.

While this history of the bicycle is inevitably an account of technological and engineering achievement, it is also a celebration of the personalities involved. There have been pioneering engineers, like James Starley of the Coventry Machinists' Company, whose Salvo tricycle attracted the attention of Queen Victoria; far-sighted inventors, like John Boyd Dunlop, a veterinary surgeon who saw the possibilities of fitting bicycles with pneumatic tyres; intrepid women, like Lady Harberton, founder of the Rational Dress Society, who took her fight against discrimination into the law courts. For over a hundred years sporting men and women have competed against each other and against the clock over a variety of distances, the most successful of them to become household names. In the great tournaments, amateur riders have been replaced by professionals sponsored by the major manufacturers, but the excitement engendered by such trials of strength as the Tour de France lives on, and with it the names of such champions as Tom Simpson and Eddie Merckx.

Now, in the 1990s, cycling has again become an important part of our lives. While the bicycle has never lost its significance as a cheap means of transport in the developing world, renewed concern for the global environment and for personal health and fitness has led to its readoption in the countries of the industrialized West. Heightened awareness of dwindling energy resources has focused attention on person-powered transport. An increasingly vocal cycling lobby campaigns for better riding conditions in the streets and for a ban on the motors that cause air and noise pollution in our city centres. The development of high-technology mountain bikes means that cross-country riding is becoming accessible to far more people than the hardy athletes of cyclo-cross sport.

Fashion has also had a part to play in this renaissance, particularly among young people. A bicycle has become a coveted possession, a symbol of freedom and pleasure in television commercials, the subject of pop music lyrics and children's films. The manufacture of designer accessories has developed into an industry of its own. The B.M.X. craze changed the face of children's bikes.

Whether this renewed interest in cycling will result in fundamental changes to future design remains to be seen. Considerations of weight and speed have continued to dominate much of the research and development taking place in the industry, although some of the most innovative ideas, such as the all-plastic Itera Cyklen of 1982, have fallen by the wayside. Nevertheless, the search for materials that are lighter, stronger and more flexible than any now available goes on.

As more motorists take the decision to abandon their cars for short journeys, there may be a greater demand for more efficient small-wheeled utility models which can be folded away for easy storage. Recumbent styles offer more comfort over long distances, but they are more difficult to manoeuvre and leave the rider feeling vulnerable, especially in heavy traffic.

It may be that our idea of the bicycle is now so closely identified with the sleek clean lines of the diamond frame that we find any other shape inappropriate and unattractive. However, given the many changes that have taken place in its development over the last two centuries, it is not unreasonable to suppose that any future history of the bicycle will look back on the present well-loved model as just another stage in its evolution.

An Age of Experimentation

An Age Of Experimentation

From the middle of the eighteenth century engineers across Europe were experimenting with man-powered vehicles. Although they toyed with three or four wheels, cranks and foot treadles, the idea of balancing on two wheels did not occur to anyone until the beginning of 1817, when Karl Drais, Freiherr Von Sauerbon (1785–1851) took out a patent on a two-wheeled machine, called the *Laufmaschine* (running machine). During 1817 the *Laufmaschine* was recognized in a number of newspaper reports and Drais published an advertising brochure about his invention. In April 1818, he devoted his energies to lecturing and to demonstrating his machine in Frankfurt while, at the same time, a servant was performing similar demonstrations at the Jardin du Luxembourg in Paris. That October, Drais himself travelled to France to show the *Laufmaschine* in Nancy and Paris.

In its crudest form the "Draisienne", as it became known to the Parisian public, consisted of a heavy bar connecting two wheels in line of roughly equal size, one behind the other, and heavy iron forks. A saddle was fixed to the bar and propulsion was achieved simply by pushing with the feet along the ground.

In the light of our modern and apparently more sophisticated standards of design, the Draisienne seems cumbersome, and yet during the early years of experimentation it represented a unique and important de-

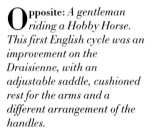

Opposite: A gentleman riding a Hobby Horse. This first English cycle was an improvement on the Draisienne, with an adjustable saddle, cushioned rest for the arms and a different arrangement of the handles.

Baron von Drais riding his Draisienne, 1818. Baron von Drais, invented this, the first rudimentary cycle, which although much ridiculed had important and lasting effects.

Training session with Hobby Horses at Johnsons's riding school in London (337 Strand and 40 Brewer Street).

velopment. By putting locomotion on two wheels, Drais had achieved a breakthrough in human transport that might be considered comparable to getting the first man on the moon; and his initial idea was adopted and exploited by many others until it was taken for granted.

Although the Draisienne fell out of favour as further technical refinements were introduced, it was a success in its own time. Drais himself gained considerable social notoriety, which ensured that his vehicles were quickly taken up in other countries, in particular the United States of America, Germany and Britain.

In 1818, Denis Johnson, a London coach-maker and entrepreneur, propagated and patented his own version of the Draisienne design, the "Pedestrian Curricle", which was soon christened the "Hobby Horse" or "Dandy Horse", as it was considered a young man's fancy. In most respects the Hobby Horse represented an improvement on the Draisienne, perhaps particularly in its more refined construction which unlike the Draisienne was steerable.

Before long it was a common sight to see young men careering along the streets or promenading through the parks on their Hobby Horses, and as they gained in popularity special riding schools were established and machines were rented out to those who could not afford to buy. Ladies' models and

Hobby Horse, 1820. The Draisienne quickly caught on in England, where it was made of iron instead of wood, and became known as the Hobby Horse.

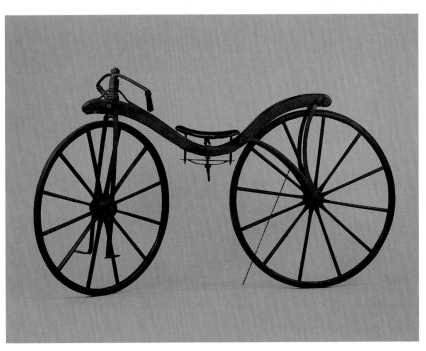

even deluxe versions were available to order. According to publications of the day well-practised persons could travel at eight, nine or even ten miles an hour on good level ground. In the crowded streets of London such speed was considered dangerous and eventually Hobby Horses were actually forbidden.

As the wheels of publicity began to turn, the tabloids of the day hunted for sensation surrounding these new machines and they found it, among the rich young men playing with their new toys. Although the Hobby Horse became a fruitful subject for carica-

Below: *Wooden bicycle built in 1818 by Nicéphore Niepce, the inventor of photography.*

Bottom: *A replica of MacMillan's machine.*

turists and satirists, it was in fact a serious machine whose true value in the evolution of the cycle can now be assessed more objectively than was possible at the time. The patent for the "Pedestrian Curricle" describes it as: "A machine for the purpose of diminishing the labour and fatigue of persons in walking and enabling them at the same time to use greater speed". The Hobby Horse narrowed distances. Given reasonable road conditions, it enabled people to travel from one village to another much more quickly than on foot. While it was a serious road vehicle to its users, it was unfortunately also a danger to the ignorant.

Indifferent to any practical considerations, the activists were only too happy to make the most of the opportunities for mockery offered them by rich young aristocrats scooting round the parks of London. Even the monarchy, in the form of the Prince Regent, did not escape their ridicule, nor did the poor old horse, apparently condemned to obsolescence by these two-wheeled fiends. While it may be more tempting to make fun of the rich than to make fun of the poor, the lower classes also rode the Hobby Horse, although they were usually unable to afford anything other than a second-hand machine.

Like any other fashion, the new vogue was short-lived. The novelty soon wore thin and the Hobby Horse disappeared, though it is hard to say whether this was due to adverse public opinion or to the drawbacks in its design. It was large, it was uncomfortable and it was heavy, yet, despite its crude construction, the Hobby Horse, like the Draisienne, was temporarily elevated to the status of a social phenomenon.

After this promising start, inventors began quietly to experiment with other types of locomotion, their aim being to construct a vehicle driven entirely by human power, without the feet touching the ground. With serious evaluation, the faults of the Hobby Horse became evident. It was not efficient: it could not convert human energy into motion. However, it could stay upright by the force of its own momentum, assuming that it was not travelling uphill or over bumpy ground.

With the advent of steam carriages and the railway, engineers became absorbed in

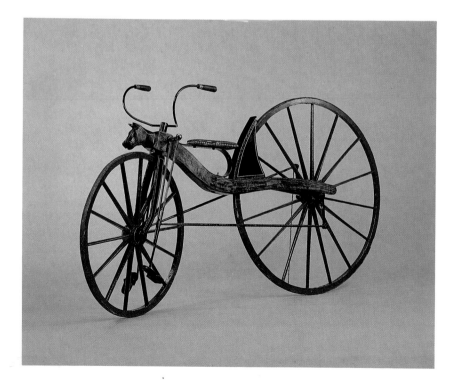

new scientific principles and abandoned the primitive technology of the Hobby Horse. A different kind of machine was needed, one that would exploit new developments in engineering and that could be ridden without crippling exertion.

After 1820 interest was again focused on vehicles with three or four wheels rather than two, and on the possibilities of treadle-drive. Although many of the inventors of this period were talented craftsmen and mechanics, the machines they designed were impractical and clumsy. Yet, even this apparently unproductive stage in the evolution of the cycle had its own importance, for it was a time of experimentation, of mechanical exploration and technological research.

However, it was not until the 1860s that inventors returned seriously to the problem of a two-wheeled man-powered machine, with one important exception. Indeed the credit for inventing the first practical pedal- or treadle-driven two-wheeled machine is generally attributed to a Scot working in the

1840s, an unassuming village blacksmith from Courthill near Dumfries, whose name was Kirkpatrick MacMillan (1813–1878). In comparison with the complicated contemporary inventions of its time, MacMillan's machine is a subtle delight.

Over the years between 1839 and 1842, MacMillan redesigned the Hobby Horse by providing it with a continuous drive to the back wheel. Unlike its precursor, his machine had a wooden frame and wooden wheels shod with iron-band tyres for strength. The two wheels ran in line and were driven by two treadles attached by connecting rods to crank arms on the back wheel. MacMillan's model is thus assumed to have been the first two-wheeled vehicle which could be driven forward without the feet touching the ground and which would remain upright through the power of its own momentum. Thus, it may be said that Mac-Millan's inventive genius had created the very first practical cycle.

MacMillan used his machine often. In 1842 he rode the gruelling 70-mile journey to

Hobby-Horses and their fashionable riders, 1818. In 1819 England experienced a Hobby-Horse craze.

Opposite: A cartoon from Punch's Almanack. 1869.

Lever-driven Quadricycle of the mid-nineteenth century.

Glasgow and, needless to say, he caused quite a stir. When he reached the Gorbals, on the outskirts of the city, a huge crowd had gathered and in the mayhem MacMillan knocked over a child. The next day he was summoned to the Police Court of Gorbals, Southside, where he was fined five shillings.

Unfortunately, MacMillan's machine has not survived and it is therefore impossible to tell what alterations were made to the original design by those craftsmen who subsequently copied it over the next twenty years. One of these, Gavin Dazell, a cooper of Lesmahagow, Lanarkshire, built his version in 1845. This machine has a curious back-

John Player cigarette card showing a Lady's Pedestrian Hobby Horse. The English developed the curved frame which allowed ladies to ride the Hobby Horse when wearing long skirts.

bone that is jointed to create two separate pieces, although the joint is a source of weakness. The pedal cranks were angled to prevent the front wheel being fouled when the machine turned. Thomas McCall, a joiner and wheelwright of Kilmarnock, also produced a version of MacMillan's original design in about 1860.

It seems surprising that rural Scotland should have been the home of these creative innovations, for it was safely tucked away from the controversy and competition over man-powered vehicles that raged in the major cities at that time. But while Mac-Millan's machine is a product of his day, it is also a fruit of the traditional craftsmanship that survived in country areas.

MacMillan did not exploit his invention; he neither advertised nor patented it. There are no contemporary diagrams or technical essays about it. His ideas never reached a wider public, and yet his creation is rightly regarded as a milestone as it anticipated the rear-driven Safety bicycle by some forty years.

A RUN WITH A RANTOONE.

THE COVER-SIDE. 10·45 A.M. SPRIGGINS COMES UP WITH THE HUNT ON HIS FAVOURITE "RANTOONE."

10·50. "FOR'ARD AWAY!" SPRIGGINS GETS ALONG FAMOUSLY.

10·56. "YOICKS!" SPRIGGINS LEARNS WHAT A "CROPPER" MEANS.

10·55. "TALLY-HO!" SPRIGGINS REALISES THE SENSATION OF BEING "RUN AWAY WITH."

11 56. FIVE MILES FROM EVERYWHERE!!

EARLY CYCLES

The 1860s bore witness to a period of intense activity in the pursuit of satisfactory personal transport. Ideas came fast and furious, changes were rapid and many avenues of research were explored, until eventually the correct solution was found. The solution was simple: a two-wheeled Velocipede; a vehicle that would carry a man forward by his own propulsion, that cost little to produce, less to keep, did not need feeding, would never bite and was light and efficient.

No one person alone can be credited with creating this machine. It should be seen as the result of an evolutionary process in design and mechanics, the pieces fitted together by a wide range of traditional craftsmen, blacksmiths, wheelwrights and coachbuilders. These men understood the importance of the Hobby Horse and experimented with the principles embodied in it. Thus, the two-wheeled Velocipede evolved and with it came a new industry, a new pastime, a new sport and an opening out of people's lives.

The first man known to have manufactured and retailed a two-wheeled Velocipede on a commercial basis was Pierre Michaux (1813–1883). A Parisian manufacturer of perambulators, invalid carriages and three-wheeled Velocipedes, Michaux was assisted by his two sons, Ernest and Henri. Like MacMillan in Scotland, Michaux also redesigned a Hobby Horse that had come into his workshop for repair, though this was in 1861, some twenty years after MacMillan's innovatory work. Michaux, however, treated the problem of man-powered vehicles in a different way from MacMillan, by attaching cranks and pedals to the front wheel as opposed to fixing treadles and cranks on the back wheel. The frame, or backbone, was of solid wrought iron, with the saddle mounted on a long, single, leaf spring. A lever shoe brake acted on the rear wheel and was applied by rotating the handlebars and tightening the attached cord. Michaux's machines were not only well-engineered, they also carried attractive detailing in the saddles, pedals, and lamp brackets.

A certain amount of controversy has always surrounded the Michaux invention, provoked by the claim of an employee of Michaux called Pierre Lallement (born 25 October 1843) from Pont-à-Mousson near Nancy, that it was he and not Michaux who invented the machine. Before entering Michaux's employ, Lallement had worked as a blacksmith in Nancy. In 1862 he had

POLICHINELLE ET SON VÉLOCIPÉDE
(MODÈLE TIRÉ DE L'ALBUM D'UN FABRICANT DE JOUETS)

Right: Cartoon from Punch, 28 August 1869. "Call it a Toy, indeed: Why our ingenious Friend, Glimmer, has a Run before Breakfast, and Grinds his Coffee and Churns his Butter with the Greatest Ease."

moved to Paris and became involved in the building of perambulators and invalid carriages. How much truth there is in Lallement's assertion is difficult to ascertain, though it may well be that he contributed to the invention even if he cannot be proved to have been its actual creator. However, the important aspect is that it *was* invented and that fact outweighs the controversy.

Leaving France in 1863/4, Lallement crossed the Atlantic to the United States where he took out a patent for a two-wheeled Velocipede. The bicycle had reached America. Inventions multiplied in the later years of the 1860s, especially in New York and Boston, and patents began to pour into the Washington patent office. Over the succeeding years, many improvements were made to the machine. As early as 1868 a New York firm, Pickering and Davis, were exporting their own machine, Pickering's improved Velocipede, to England.

In England, the "American Bicycle", as it became known, was distributed by Messrs Samuel & Pearce of Liverpool. Advertisements of the period stated that American Velocipedes were stronger and more desirable than English or French machines, and claimed that they would outlast their English and French cousins. Pickering's Velocipede incorporated one intriguing new feature: a

CALL IT A TOY, INDEED! WHY, OUR INGENIOUS FRIEND, GLIMMER, HAS A RUN BEFORE BREAKFAST, AND GRINDS HIS COFFEE AND CHURNS HIS BUTTER WITH THE GREATEST EASE.

swept back handlebar. This could be seen as a design fault as it forced the rider's arms into a position too near to his chest. In addition the saddle was unsprung and a curious braking system required the rider to push down onto the saddle in order to apply the brake to the back wheel. In America, as in France and Britain, those people responsible for introducing improvements to existing machines were blacksmiths, wheelwrights, foundrymen and other craftsmen.

As the Velocipede gained in popularity, riding schools soon appeared and publications were written to teach the fine art of Velocipede-riding. When America unofficially declared 1869 the year of the Velocipede, a dozen or so songs were published, dedicated to the new hobby and sport. The "Velocipede Galop", by Henry B. Hart, published by C.H. Ditson of New York, was one of these. Its cover illustration daringly shows a lady wearing bloomers and sitting astride a Velocipede. A woman also features on the cover of the "Velocipede Set, March and Galop" by E. Mack, published by Lee and Walker of Philadelphia, although she is modestly dressed in flowing skirts. After this initial fervour, however, the Velocipede craze had died in America by the end of 1871. Fashions had changed and the new machine simply fell out of favour.

After two years Lallement left the United States and returned to Paris where a fresh

Michaux Velocipede, 1868. Michaux's order books show that in 1861 he built two machines, in 1862 this went up to 142 and by 1865 it was more than 400.

A Transitional Velocipede, early 1870s.

impetus was brought to the development of the bicycle. The year 1867 was important because of the Paris exhibition when the machine was introduced to the public for the first time, with considerable success. As a result Michaux's business expanded at home and he was able to begin exporting his products to England. Any demand that Michaux was unable to satisfy was taken up by others that went into the business. Thus, from 1867 onwards competition raged, as exploitation of the machine afforded moneymaking opportunities to new companies. Sadly, after his tremendous initial success, Michaux himself came to a sorry end. Having sold his rights to the Compagnie Parisienne, he had started up again on his own, but an ensuing lawsuit eventually ruined him and he died destitute and insane in a Paris hospital.

As the Velocipede caught the public's imagination it became increasingly popular and was soon a social institution. To ride a Velocipede was an accomplishment comparable to riding a horse or dancing. Riding schools were set up and machines could be hired out. With the establishment of the first Velocipeding clubs in Paris, what had previously been a hobby became a serious pastime boasting organized races. The first recorded track race was ridden on 31 May 1868 at St Cloud, near Paris, over a distance of 1,200 metres, and was won by James Moore, an Englishman living in France. Then on 9 November in the following year,

Prince Louis-Napoléon on his Michaux cycle, accompanied by his cousin.

the first road race was held between Paris and Rouen, a distance of 123 kilometres. This was a remarkable race, for there were 323 entries, and of the 100 who actually started at least four were women riders, who were more than willing to compete against men. In the cycling world at least, emancipation for women fought its way to the forefront much earlier in France than in Britain. Many different types of machines entered the race, including monocycles, tricycles and quadricycles. The undisputed victor was again James Moore, who arrived in Rouen in only 10¾ hours, having ridden at an average speed of nearly twelve kilometres an hour.

However, the authorities did not appreciate the Velocipede. Regarding it as nothing more than a nuisance, officials banned it from the streets and restricted its use to parks. Far from deterring the riders, this only strengthened their resolve. Like the modern bicycle of today, the Velocipede cut across all social barriers and was adopted by upper and lower classes, by both men and women, all of whom appreciated the advantages of independent mobility.

The Velocipedes ridden by women were different inasmuch as they were ridden side-saddle and dress-guards were added to pro-tect the skirts of the riders from becoming entangled with the front and rear spokes. Eventually it became clear to those French ladies who had taken to the Velocipede that skirts were unsuitable for riding. Instead, they wore what was later to be known as Rational dress, when its advocates tried to popularize it in the 1890s. Riding comfort-ably and impressively about in their tights and knickerbockers, Parisian women must have seemed immodest and immoral in the eyes of many British people.

As the use of the Velocipede spread to such a broad range of the public, it was inevitable that the press would satirize this new phenomenon. With much of the popula-tion of Paris perched precariously on two wheels, the Velocipede became a natural topic for ridicule and was much caricatured.

Eventually, it was necessary to make im-provements to the initial model in order to retain the interest of this new market. Unfortunately the advent of the Franco-Prussian War interrupted this fledgling in-dustry and the factories were taken over for weapon production. One side effect of the war, however, was that, while manufacture of the Velocipede ground to a virtual halt in France, it was taken up by other countries, especially England, where the market was

Opposite above: The training school for cyclists, Paris 1869.

Opposite below: A velocipede riding school in New York. Harper's Weekly, 13 February 1869. In 1869 rinks, halls and riding schools were opened in rapid succession in many American cities.

The English Boneshaker, early 1870s. After the Franco-Prussian war, the initiative in cycle manufacture and design passed from France to England, where the public was extremely enthusiastic about the 'boneshaker'.

cultivated and expanded, even if the English regarded the new craze in a sedate, less boisterous, fashion.

The manufacture was not concentrated in one particular area but spread throughout the country, from London to Liverpool, to Wolverhampton and especially to Coventry which became a major centre of bicycle production when the Coventry Sewing Machine Company was among the first to become involved in the new industry. In 1868, the sewing machine trade was slack and the firm decided to make Velocipedes for sale in France, changing its name to the Coventry Machinists' Company Limited in order to accommodate the diversification. An initial order for 200 machines was cancelled due to the progression of the Franco-Prussian War, but the company managed to offset this loss of market by developing a domestic trade in bicycles. This one event is reputed to have sparked off the Coventry

cycle industry. Now, precision had taken over from craft. The shift from the smithy to the professional builder saw the demise of the individual craftsman and the rise of an industry.

In England the Velocipede was nicknamed the "Boneshaker" because of the jarring effect caused to the rider when travelling over uneven roads. Riders were treated with derision and terror. A new venture always has its critics. Labelled dangerous by the press, who did not fully understand its achievements, the Boneshaker, like its French cousin, came in for its own share of satirical comment and fun-poking caricature. Many appeared in magazines such as *Punch*, which created humour by commenting on social habits.

Again, riders of the new vehicle represented a broad spectrum of society. As with any fashionable mania, those who could afford to indulged in cycle-riding. Bicycle clubs were formed and the many members began to ride great distances, even going from London to John o'Groats. The first organized race in England was held in a field near Welsh Harp, Hendon, on Whit Monday, 1868. The gentlemen Boneshaker rider

"With a proper teacher of their own sex, and with suitable dresses for the preliminary practice, ladies can obtain such a command over the velocipedes in one week's practice, of an hour daily, that they can ride side-saddle-wise with the utmost ease."—*New York Sun.*

OH! THEN, THIS IS WHAT WE MAY EXPECT TO SEE THIS SEASON.

generally wore a billycock hat or a boater, although no particular costume was favoured until later in the 1870s and 1880s when club bicyclists became very keen on uniform. Then, the polo cap or pillbox were amazingly popular although they gave little or no protection from the rain or the sun.

Towards the end of 1870 a transitional period occurred. With heightened success there came greater scope for invention. As the machine began to be used increasingly for longer journeys, greater speeds and more efficiency were needed, and consumer demand led to improvements being introduced. One of the design adaptations of this period was to make the front (driving) wheel larger so that more ground could be covered with each revolution of the pedal. The seat was also brought forward so that the rider was positioned more directly over the pedals and could thus use his weight more effectively in direct motion with his legs. Wider handlebars improved the steering column.

By the close of the 1870 season the Boneshaker was becoming obsolete and interest in it was confined only to a few racing men and touring club enthusiasts. Its place in public favour was taken over by the elegant and much faster High Wheeler, later to be known as the Ordinary Bicycle.

The American Velocipede, 1868. Enthusiasm for the velocipede in America was very short-lived and up-until 1876 the bicycle had a limited use there.

Opposite above: A cycle race, 1869.

Opposite below: The first cycle race for ladies in France. Bordeaux, 1 November 1868.

Left: A cartoon from Punch, 18 May 1869. "Oh! Then, this is what we may expect to see this season."

THE ORDINARY

Elegant, simple, efficient, and perhaps a little precarious, the Ordinary developed from the Velocipede as a response to the need for speed, lightness of design, better performances and greater comfort. As the front wheel grew larger, there was a corresponding reduction in the size of the rear wheel in order to lessen the overall weight of the machine. The result of these changes was known as the "Ordinary" or "High" Bicycle, later to be given the unkind name of "Penny Farthing".

Between 1870 and 1878 scores of patents were taken out for this design and scores more for improvements, such as rigid spoking systems, front-operated rear brakes, seat springs, pedals and the general adoption of ball bearings for the wheel spindles.

The first all-metal English bicycle to be mass-produced was called the "Ariel". It weighed about 50 lb. and retailed at £8, which was not particularly expensive for the well-to-do but was equivalent to eight times the average man's wage. Patented by James Starley on 11 August 1870, the "Ariel" was made under licence by Haynes and Jeffries and remained in production for nearly ten years. It was the first machine to incorporate the centre-steering head and "lever tension" wheels, in which the radial spokes were held taut by a pair of levers attached to the hubs and the rims.

By 1874 there were some twenty firms making bicycles in England, mainly in Coventry, Birmingham and London. The pioneering manufacturers included James Starley; William Hillman; Dan Rudge; W.H.J. Grout, who in 1871 devised his own version of the tension wheel by individual adjustment of each radial spoke by a nipple at the rim; Fred Cooper; and George Singer, whose "Challenge" was one of the more popular mounts of 1876. Starley, Hillman and Singer had all been employed by the Coventry Machinists' Company before they left to form their own companies.

The Coventry Machinists' Company itself made great strides in improving the bicycle and for several years their "Gentleman's" bicycle (originally called the "Spider") was considered the height of perfection. However, by 1878 the "Club Model" had succeeded the "Gentleman's" to become the Coventry Machinists' Company classic touring machine combining speed and utility with beauty. The frame was made of tapered oval steel and the spine closely followed the curve of the front wheel. All the components, including rims, were refined and made hollow to save unnecessary weight.

Although the Ordinary was ridden primarily by young, middle-class men, women too had their own design of the bicycle. In 1874, Starley produced an "Ariel" specifically for ladies. It had a side-saddle, such as that designed for the ladies' Boneshaker,

Opposite: *A Penny Farthing.*

Advertisement from the Illustrated London News, July 21, 1888. Coventry swapped its tradition of pin manufacture for the new cycle-building industry, and from 1870–90 cycles of every shape and size were produced there.

The Ordinary High Wheeler.

Right: Display of dexterity on penny-farthings in Tuileries Gardens, Paris, 1875.

and the pedals drove cranks through levers which were pivoted in front of, and slightly above, the front wheel axle. Connecting rods communicated the pedal motion to the overhung crank shaft.

Because of the side-saddle position, the handlebars were shortened on one side and lengthened on the other. The rear wheel was mounted on an overhung axle instead of the usual arrangement of a spindle carried within a fork. The track of the front wheel was offset from that of the rear wheel to counteract the bias from the side-saddle position.

Even so, bicycling was still a sport for athletic young men, who were proud of the scars they incurred in mastering their mechanical steeds, since once mastered the Ordinary moved with a smooth, graceful motion. Many of these young men joined clubs to pursue their pastime, and soon the Ordinary became a cult among a huge body of bicyclists.

By 1878 there were approximately 64 clubs in London alone and a further 125 in the provinces. These institutions offered companionship as well as a forum of common interests, and many joined for the social life they afforded. The larger clubs had 100 or more members, and taking into account both these numbers and the many thousands more who did not join a club, it is

possible to appreciate the popularity of the bicycle. Club bicyclists adopted certain codes of behaviour, and tended to be snobbish towards non-members. Many of these lone cyclists were slaves to fashion, wearing tight tunics buttoned up to the neck, with padding at the shoulders, heavily braided in military style, and tight braided breeches which buttoned under the knee. Accessories included gauntlets which reached halfway up the arms, long stockings and shoes, top boots or hunting boots. However, not everyone felt it was necessary to have special clothes just for riding. The working classes still found it difficult to afford the bicycles alone, prices of which represented several weeks' wages. One of the main reasons why the club members ridiculed their less fortunate fellows who had not joined appears to have been that they considered them untidy-looking. The club cyclists rode in their own uniform of tight knickerbocker suits, in dark colours so the dirt from the road did not show, and pillbox caps which displayed the badge of their club at the front. At meetings, the club bugler would sound a few

notes to summon the riders before they set off together on their club run.

Bicycle clubs also developed rapidly in France and to some extent in America. America had previously suffered a lull in enthusiasm for bicycling after the Velocipede had fallen completely out of favour, so much so that when the Ordinary was exported to New England in 1877 it was extremely slow to take off. Manufacturing in the United States did not begin until a year later with the Pope Manufacturing Company in Hartford, Connecticut, and in the same year the first club was founded in America – The Boston Bicycle Club.

Now that the means to do so had become available, people were getting out and about, exploring the countryside and widening their experience. The bicycle was also acting as a social leveller. Given independent transport, working men could move out to the suburbs and pursue a healthy lifestyle with their families. At the same time, bicycling as a sport was growing increasingly popular. Ordinary racing drew huge crowds in the 1880s, establishing its own idols for

The Ariel Ordinary, c. 1876.

the period, and there was often heavy betting on the outcome of the races. Around half a dozen periodicals dealing with the sport were produced in England alone.

The tracks were generally made of ash and cinders and measured ¼ mile (440 yards) or sometimes less in circumference. Spectators either stood outside the track or, at larger grounds, could sit in the stands. The central area was restricted to judges, stewards and other officials and there was usually a large board on which details of the current race were displayed as well as results of previous events. Sport tracks of this kind were to be found both inside and outside the capital such as at Herne Hill, Canning Town, Crystal Palace and numerous other places.

Most manufacturers produced a racing model which might weigh as little as 25 lb., whereas a 50-inch tourer could weigh up to 50 lb. The companies exhibited their wares at annual cycle shows, the first of which, the Stanley Bicycle Club Cycle Show, was held in 1878.

After 1878 new models were produced at frequent intervals. One example is the "Matchless" of 1883, whose design marked a further technical advance in construction. Weight was reduced by means of steel tubing for both the front forks and the frame, and the use of hollow rims for the wheels. Overall

Opposite: An advertisement for the Columbia bicycle, 1895.

Right: An advertisement for the Columbia bicycle.

Below: Advertisement from Frank Leslie's Illustrated Newspaper, 3 May 1879. In 1878, the Pope Manufacturing Company, of which Col. Albert A. Pope was president, started manufacturing their own bicycle, the 'Columbia', which was an excellent and practical machine. This first good American bicycle, entitles Mr Pope to the name of pioneer manufacturer of the modern bicycle in America.

COLUMBIA BICYCLE.

We commence this season with four patterns of bicycles; three of them, the Special, Ordinary, and Youth's, entirely new, and our old Columbia in its improved form, which we now call the Standard.

The prices of these vary from $50 to $150, according to the size, quality, and finish of the machine, and are suited to the heights, tastes, and means of all purchasers.

Having had two years' experience in the manufacture of bicycles, and the benefit of all the best English machines to guide us, we now claim to make the best finished and most durable bicycle ever put upon the market in any country.

We keep the largest stock and best assortment of bicycle sundries of any dealer in the country.

Send 3-cent stamp for Catalogue and Price-list, containing full information, to

THE POPE M'F'G CO.

87 Summer Street . . Boston, Mass.

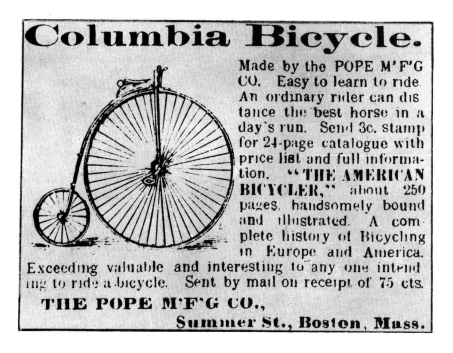

Columbia Bicycle.

Made by the POPE M'F'G CO. Easy to learn to ride. An ordinary rider can distance the best horse in a day's run. Send 3c. stamp for 24-page catalogue with price list and full information. "THE AMERICAN BICYCLER," about 250 pages, handsomely bound and illustrated. A complete history of Bicycling in Europe and America. Exceeding valuable and interesting to any one intending to ride a bicycle. Sent by mail on receipt of 75 cts.

THE POPE M'F'G CO.,
Summer St., Boston, Mass.

performance was further improved by the use of ball bearings.

Wider acceptance of the Ordinary also led to rapid development of a variety of components and accessories. Tyres were initially made from solid rubber or leather. The rubber tyre had wire running all the way through the centre, which ensured it was secured firmly to the rim. Leather tyres were constructed in four metal-backed pieces and were fixed to the rim by screws. Later types of tyre were made of spongy rubber, and after John Boyd Dunlop's innovatory work of 1888 some bicycles were even fitted with pneumatic tyres.

Handlebars were at first straight, but later, as the front wheel became larger, they were dropped in design. Handlegrips were rounded handles usually made from horn or rosewood. A great variety of saddles was produced to meet the general desire for greater ease and comfort. There were also many different kinds of brake, most of them based on rods or rollers applied to the rear wheel. By 1880 the front brake, introduced by John Kean in 1873, had been more generally adopted because of its greater power. The spoon, or roller, was activated by hand-levers on the handlebars and through rods. This allowed the rider to coast downhill with his legs over the handlebars, although most bicyclists preferred to dismount when a hill appeared too steep.

Many Ordinary riders had some form of road warning device, in the shape of a bell, gong or whistle. There was also a variety of candle and oil lamps, designed to be carried either on the front forks or on the hub of the front wheel. The hub lamp was suspended by means of an integral bearing on the hub of the front wheel and within the spokes.

However, not all the bicyclist's problems could be so easily solved. Despite the introduction of so many fittings designed to give a safer and more comfortable ride, the actual roads were extremely neglected and in a poor state of repair. On such surfaces it was difficult to maintain stability, and a heavy fall forward over the handlebars could be fatal, although most riders learned to fall correctly.

The Bicycle Touring Club was founded by Stanley John Ambrose Cotterell, a medical student who was interested in long-distance

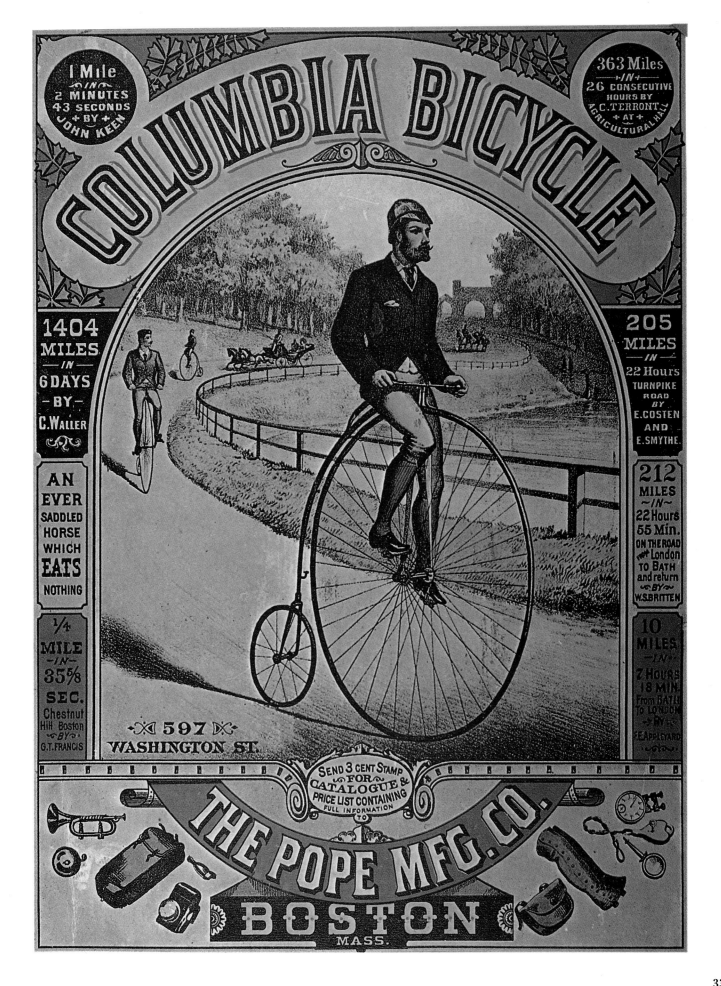

travel. Through letters in cycling magazines, Cotterell formed contacts with other keen cyclists, such as T. Hyram Holding of Sunderland and George Lacy Hillier of Chichester. Their correspondence covered several topics, including road conditions, routes and the idea of forming an organization to provide information to cyclists. S.H. Inecon suggested in one letter to *Bicycling Times* that they ought to put their theories into practice. So on 5 August 1878 Cotterell rode his Ordinary from his home in Edinburgh to a Bank Holiday meeting of bicyclists in Harrogate, where he met his fellow enthusiasts and the Bicycle Touring Club was founded with fifty members. Cotterell was made Honorary Secretary, a position he relinquished in the late summer of 1879 to W. Wellford, who became the first paid official. Cotterell was elected the first president of the club.

By 1880 the Bicycle Touring Club had 3,000 members and the *Gazette* magazine was founded, which provided a countrywide list of dangerous hills. In that year the Bicycle Touring Club also played host to a group of American cyclists in Liverpool, and when these visitors returned home they formed the L.A.W., the League of American Wheelmen.

During this period the Bicycle Touring

Club adopted a uniform which was slightly modified each season to follow new trends in colour and cut. Thus, a dark green Devonshire serge straight jacket, with matching knickerbockers and grey stockings, gave way in 1880 to a Norfolk jacket, green stockings and white gloves. However, so many complaints were made about the uniform that the club was obliged to appoint a committee to look into the whole question. In a response dated 1882, the club stated that it would obtain its own grey checked cloth and appoint its own tailors. Over the following years, however, there continued to be changes in the style of dress. Knee-breeches, or knickerbockers were all worn at various times, and, under the influence of prevailing fashions, often with gaiters. Even the hats altered from one season to the next. Helmets were popular, either a soft variety or a stiff design which was waterproofed with cork. Later, cricket caps were preferred to the polo or jockey cap. These were made of flannel and were stiff, peaked and unlined.

In 1883, the Bicycle Touring Club changed its name to The Cyclists' Touring Club, so that it could include tricyclists. At the same time parallel organizations were formed on the Continent, including the Touring Club Italiano, the Touring Club

The emblem of the Buffalo Bicycle Club – 'The bicycle adds wings to the foot'. This club was organised on 22 February, 1879 and had 10 members then.

The first national meeting of American bicyclists at Newport, Rhode Island, 31 May, 1880. From Frank Leslie's Illustrated Newspaper, June 19, 1880. Due to Pope's enthusiasm bicycling became one of the most popular sports in America.

Left: *Maps and cyclometers.*

Below: *Warning devices.*

Belgique, the Touring Club Suisse and the Touring Club France.

The change of name, however, did nothing to resolve the continuing arguments regarding cycling costume. Women were becoming increasingly anxious about their cumbersome clothes, and in January 1884 the uniform question was again raised at a ladies' meeting of the Cyclists' Touring Club. It was generally felt that a ladies' club dress was a necessity. The Rational Dress Association might have been called upon to suggest a suitable model, but at this early stage in its development it provoked little excitement.

During this period the ladies could be divided into three categories: those who endorsed the need for some form of special dress, those who were content with modified and reasonable departures from the garments in general use, and those who favoured a pronounced and thoroughly different costume. Many women argued that

Top: *N.C.U. Official Quarters sign.*

Middle: *N.C.U. danger sign.*

Bottom: *C.T.C. winged sign.*

Right: *The road rules put forward by the Bicycle Union of America in 1879.*

RECOMMENDATIONS IN REGARD TO ROAD-RIDING.

1. It is desirable that a rider should at all times keep to the left-hand side of the road, even if no vehicle be in sight; and riding on the footway should never be resorted to. The rules of the road should be strictly adhered to: i.e., in meeting any vehicle or rider, always keep to the left; in overtaking any thing which is going in the same direction as the rider, pass on the right; but, on meeting or passing a led horse, take that side of the road on which the man is who is leading the animal.

2. Under no circumstances should a rider pass on the wrong side of a vehicle; as, in the event of an accident, he thereby renders himself liable for damages.

3. Before overtaking any passenger on the road, a signal should be given, and whilst at a sufficient distance to allow such passenger time to look round before the rider passes.

4. On no account pass between two riders when overtaking them: riders, upon hearing a signal from any man wishing to pass, should take close order to the left, and, if the road be narrow, take order in single file.

5. On forming single from double file, the right-hand man should fall to the rear of his companion.

6. In turning a corner the rider should moderate his pace, and should give a signal, unless he can see a sufficient distance ahead to be assured that no vehicle is near, and that no foot-passenger is crossing or about to cross.

7. In turning a corner to the right [see note], care should be taken to leave sufficient room for any vehicle to pass on its own side, as some drivers are particularly fond of swinging round a corner at a fast pace.

8. Foot-passengers on the road should not be needlessly shouted at, but should be courteously warned, and be given a wide berth, especially at crossings.

9. Care should be taken by the bicyclist not to startle any horse by passing at a high rate of speed; and, upon meeting one which shows signs of restiveness, a dismount should invariably be made, if requested by the driver, and in as quiet a manner as possible: it is, however, frequently desirable to ride slowly by, speaking to the horse, as a sudden dismount might frighten the animal.

10. The ground in front of a horse should not be taken until the bicyclist is at least ten yards ahead.

11. In company riding, (*a*) The leader, on passing any one, should announce that others are following. (*b*) The leader should, at all times, give sufficient notice to allow those in the rear to slacken speed, before easing up himself. (*c*) When descending a hill, the machine should be kept thoroughly under control, and riders should not rush past those preceding them, with feet off the pedals.

12. For night riding, a lamp should be used to signify to other passengers the whereabouts of the bicyclist; and in frequented thoroughfares warning should be given by bell, or in some noticeable manner, of his otherwise noiseless approach.

their skirts were too full and freedom of movement was restricted. In answer to their pleas, the Rational Dress Assocation eventually approved what they felt to be the basic requirements of any new ladies' uniform, including an even distribution of weight and warmth over the body, an assurance of freedom of movement and the avoidance of any obtrusive appearance. As one member stated: "A lady should inwardly dress like a gentleman, but outwardly like a lady".

Long loose trousers offered one solution and there were strong advocates for the divided skirt. However, having given all aspects of the problem due consideration, members finally agreed upon an overskirt and Norfolk jacket made from Cyclist' Touring Club cloth or flannel. Accessories included a hat, also made of the club material or of straw with the club ribbon, and black woollen stockings. On this occasion, the Rational Dress Association had been defeated, but it had at least provoked some response and was to continue balloting and petitioning until it met with greater success in the bicycling heyday of the 1890s.

When E. Shipton become Honorary Secretary of the Club in 1883, he introduced new measures concerning road safety and road construction, and the Cyclists' Touring Club campaigned both locally and nationally for road signs. The Bicycle Union (later the National Cyclists' Union or N.C.U.) had already led the way by erecting danger boards. These took the form of stout iron plates measuring 18 inches by 13 inches. The fronts of the plates were white enamel with "Dangerous" painted on them in red and any other words in black. The boards had been supplied free to anyone willing to pay for erecting them and were fixed at no less than ten feet from the level of the road. In 1887 the Cyclists' Touring Club and the N.C.U. passed a joint resolution to erect warning signs on top of dangerous hills. This arrangement lasted until 1897 when the Cyclists' Touring Club were left to carry on the work alone. Finally, in 1903 the Motor Car Act was passed and this provided for the erection of road signs by county councils.

By 1886, membership of the Cyclists' Touring Club had reached 21,000 and was still rising. That year also saw the introduction of the Winged Wheel emblem, which

was awarded to hostelries providing services for cyclists as a mark of the club's approval.

From 1900 to 1914 there was a slow decline in the number of cyclists due to an increase in the popularity of motoring. It is ironic, perhaps, that the improvements in road conditions which made safe driving for motor vehicles possible would never have come about had cycling not been so widely taken up. Shipton even wanted the word "Cyclists" dropped from the club name so that the organization could include motor vehicles too, but his proposal was dismissed in a postal ballot and he left his post to pursue his motoring interests. In 1910 King George V conferred royal patronage upon the Cyclists' Touring Club, and this has been renewed ever since.

George Herbert Stancer was made secretary in 1920, a post he held until 1945. Stancer was a tireless campaigner for the rights of cyclists and he instituted the legal department which gave free assistance to members. From the beginning of the First World War to the close of the Second, the Cyclists' Touring Club produced a series of papers on such topics as rear lights, cycle taxation and cycling safety in the school curriculum. By the 1970s an increase in environmental concerns had boosted the membership again and touring was no longer

The 60 inch Ordinary, c. 1880.

confined mainly to the British counties and to Europe, but had expanded to include Third World countries as well. Today, tour programmes are arranged in such places as Thailand, Peru, Venezuela and the United States. The Cyclists' Touring Club now boasts over 40,000 members, with 200 affiliated clubs and 200 groups nationwide.

Before the foundation of its predecessor, the Bicycle Touring Club, however, bicycling was not taken seriously by the public. Remarking that it was dangerous, many did

Cartoon from Punch, 6 December, 1879. "The Line of Beauty."

THE LINE OF BEAUTY.

Athletic. "DON'T YOU BICYCLE?"

Æsthetic. "ER—NO. IT DEVELOPES THE CALVES OF THE LEGS SO! MAKES 'EM STICK OUT, YOU KNOW! SO COARSE! POSITIVE DEFORMITY!!"

not appreciate the unprecedented extent to which it had opened out people's lives. Riders were ridiculed and physically abused in the streets. There was confusion as to their legal status and their rights on public roads. Bicyclists were not to ride on footpaths, they had to use a light after dark and to ring a bell continuously to warn others of their presence. In Coventry a six-mile-an-hour speed limit was enforced for bicyclists. The bicycling literature of the period was full of complaints by riders who had been barged into hedges by horse-driven vehicles or tripped up by "Country Louts". With the formation of the Bicycle Touring Club, the bicycle succeeded in acquiring a legal definition and the rights of bicyclists were defended openly.

Although the Ordinary gave a great impetus to the bicycle industry and encouraged the spread of the bicycling movement, it was finally superseded. Many of its supporters were reluctant to see it go. As alternative designs, such as tricycles and experimental Safeties, began to appear towards the close of the 1870s, the athletic young men who had championed the Ordinary continued to defend it. For other would-be riders, however, among them the not-so-young, the less physically fit and women of all ages, the Ordinary was a much less practical proposition. To mount it the rider had to scoot forward with the right leg, while the left foot remained on the mounting step. When the rider had gained enough momentum, he slipped forward onto the saddle and then began pedalling. Once in motion, the high centre of gravity located near the steering axis also caused the machine to be comparatively unstable.

Speed was another, although less important factor in the disappearance of the Ordinary. In its time it had represented a considerable improvement on the Boneshaker. In 1884 for example, Thomas Stevens rode around the world in the impressive time of two and a half years, and before that, in 1882, Herbert Lidell Cortis had ridden just over 20 miles in one hour. The son of a South London doctor, Cortis was born in Filey, Yorkshire, in 1857. Eventually entering Guy's Hospital as a medical student, he rode as a member of the Wanderers Bicycle Club. Although his En-

glish racing career lasted only five years' Cortis achieved many admirable results. On 16 June 1877, he won a five-mile handicap race with a handicap of 350 yards. The following year he won the club mile with a handicap of 10 yards in a time of 3 minutes 26 seconds, on a rough grass track. Cortis then began to take part in open events. In 1879 he was the first man to win all four National Cyclists' Union Championships (1 mile, 5 miles, 25 miles, and 50 miles). A fine, strong young man, his height of 6 feet 2½ inches enabled him to ride machines with 58-inch and 60-inch wheels. In 1882 Cortis, newly married, sailed for Australia where he continued to race until two days before he died at the age of 28 from complications following a fall from a horse.

Even record speeds such as these were no longer considered fast enough. After 1885 the runaway success of the Rover rear-driven Safeties began to affect the sales of Ordinaries. Other manufacturers fought back by making their own "safe" machine. Known as the Rational it had a large hind wheel, 22–26 inches as against 16–18 inches, more rake to the front forks and more clearance between the tyre and the back-bone. However, this design only delayed the inevitable.

The demise of the Ordinary marked the end of an era in bicycling history. They ceased to excel after 1892, after which time manufacturing virtually ceased.

Left: *An American bicyclist.*

Below: *Starley's bicycle, nicknamed the Spider, 1872.*

ALTERNATIVE MOUNTS:
TRICYCLES AND SOCIABLES

During the years between 1860 and 1870 there was so much excitement over the Ordinary and its improvements that for many there seemed little point in alternative possibilities. However, the fact remained that it was really only suitable for the strong, young, male rider. If others were to be given the freedom of independent locomotion, it was necessary to reconsider the problems of instability that arose from having to balance on two wheels and experiment with three or four instead.

The earliest forms of tricycle were modified Velocipedes and appeared in France, the United States and Britain soon after their two-wheeled cousins. Driven directly by means of cranks and pedals, these machines had two smaller rear wheels running free to an axle fitted to the end of the backbone. The French designs in particular demonstrated the graceful lines that were found in so many of the two-wheeled Velocipedes. The French also led the way in tricycle-racing, which began earlier in France than in Britain, and came to be a well-loved and well-attended sport. During 1869–70, there were organized races in 159 cities and towns, of which all except London, Birmingham, Brussels and Madrid were French.

Although men found the Velocipede tricycle easy to ride, the presence of the backbone made it more difficult for women. However, by the late 1870s velocipede tricycles were adapted to treadle-drive, in which levers transferred the power to a cranked axle. Even when wearing their voluminous skirts, women were able to ride these models with as much enthusiasm as the men.

Whereas France had led the way with the development of the front-driven two-wheeled Velocipede, it was in Ireland that the first practical tricycle design was patented. This early machine was designed by William Blood of Dublin, who patented his model in November 1876, and it was built by the Carey Brothers, also of Dublin. The machine had a large rear driving-wheel with two smaller steering-wheels in front mounted in separate forks. The rear wheel was driven by wooden treadles.

During 1877 and 1878 there were applications for a further fifty-seven patents regarding tricycles, but the early years of manufacture and design came to be dominated by one man, James Starley of Coventry (1830–1881). Starley is still revered as the "Father of the Cycle Industry" and no history of the cycle would be complete without a tribute to him. A gifted and natural inventor, he is reputed to have been the first man to put the tricycle successfully into full-scale production.

Born of country stock at Albourne, Sussex, Starley received only a basic education and was put to work at an early age on his father's farm. After a variety of jobs, including gardener, labourer and spare time mechanic to a number of people, he managed to obtain a position with a London firm of sewing machine makers. Finally, he

Opposite: The French Army of Velocipedistes, 1888.

A John Player cigarette card of the Coventry Rotary Tricycle. This was a two track machine, the big wheel on the left being the driver. The two small wheels were steered by the handle which the rider held in his right hand.

moved to Coventry, where he gained employment with the European Sewing Machine Company, later to become famous as the Coventry Machinists' Company, attributed to be the first manufacturers of the English Velocipede.

Starley, it seems, was not a person to rest content with reproducing other inventors' designs, but worked to improve construction of the Velocipede to match his own ideals and standards. Having patented the "Ariel" (with William Hillman) in 1871, Starley went on to introduce new designs, lighter yet stronger constructional materials, and to revolutionize the existing design of steering-head.

Business was successful and Starley turned his thoughts to the timid or less agile rider who complained of being unable or unwilling to achieve independent mobility on the precarious Ordinary. His solution was to re-design the unsuccessful lever-driven ladies' Ariel Ordinary. This he did by lowering the position of the rider, placing a driving-wheel on one side and two smaller wheels on the other, while still retaining lever-drive. The "Coventry Lever Tricycle", as Starley's new machine was called, was an immediate success, and was first sold under licence by Haynes and Jeffries in March 1877. To begin with it was steered by a handle connected to the small wheel. The left fork of this wheel was in turn connected to the right fork of the rear wheel. A rack-and-pinion system soon replaced the handle, a chain-drive was added and the machine became known as the "Coventry Rotary Tricycle".

The Coventry Rotary Tricycle proved to be a very popular mount. Advertisements emphasized its versatility, and in 1889 it was claimed that: "It is the only machine for the photographer, artist, sportsman, angler or surveyor, the long side tube affording facility for carriage of photographic apparatus, easel, gun, fishing-rod or tripod".

During May 1877, Starley added another large wheel and an extra crank. This new machine was further improved by the removal of the small rear wheel so that two riders, seated side by side, could pedal independently, each driving the side wheel nearest to him. Starley had transformed the lever tricycle into the first "Sociable".

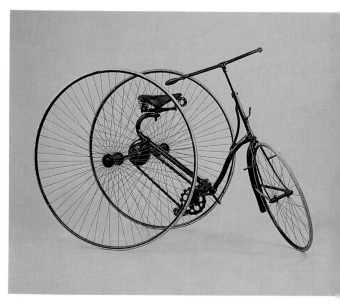

The new design proved difficult to handle, however, because the power exerted on the two wheels varied constantly, and consequently it was hard to steer the vehicle in a straight line. The solution to this problem was patented and developed as part of the Salvoquadricycle in September 1877. It was called the "balance gear" or "double driving gear", later to be known as the "differential gear". As with many other ingenious inventions, there is some contention as to whether Starley was the author of the differential gear. There is said to be at least one French patent for it, taken out by Onesime Pecquer in 1828. What matters, though, is not so much who invented it, but that Starley applied it.

Above right: *Coventry Front Drive Tricycle, c. 1870s–80s. The problem of balancing on a velocipede was still a serious obstacle to the general acceptance of cycles. With the advent of the tricycle the cyclist could remain seated even when stationary.*

Below right: *Sparkbrook Tricycle, early 1880s. Tricycles particularly appealed to ladies and elderly gentlemen. The term 'tricycle' first occurred in the French patent to Ducausais, in 1828.*

Bottom: *The Salvo Sociable of 1882, ridden by Mr and Mrs Welford. In 1939 Mrs Welford became the first woman member of the C.T.C.*

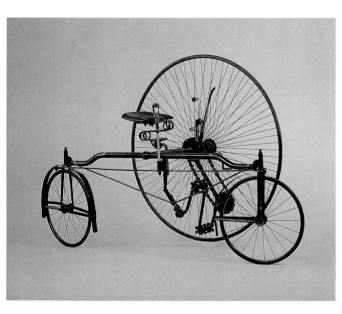

weight version. In 1880 a Miss Roach riding a Salvo was seen by Queen Victoria, who summoned her to appear at Osborne House. As a result Her Majesty ordered two of the tricycles, and the Salvo became known as the "Royal Salvo".

Starley applied his inventive powers to a variety of problems during the course of his career. He patented designs for all manner of articles, from brakes and bath chairs, and from hand lever machines for riders who had lost the use of their legs, to a tricycle that could be folded up for storage purposes called the "Compressus". The last patent he took out, in the spring of 1881, was for an improved folding tricycle and this machine was marketed by Messrs Singer & Company, Coventry, as the "Challenge". The 1880 price list for the "Challenge" describes its mechanism quite clearly, as one "which enables the machine to pass through any ordinary doorway". On 17 June 1881, Starley died of cancer, having gained only a modest fortune and minor fame. An unassuming man who loved mechanics, he was well respected by his workforce and his contemporaries.

Between 1860 and 1895 many new designs came onto the market, to be replaced by yet more, as fashions changed. Apart from the tricycle, other alternative mounts to the bicycle included dicycles and quadricycles, both of which were also produced in tandem or sociable versions.

There were several attempts to make a single-wheeled monocycle, but without much practical success. The first proposal for a dicycle, a machine with two wheels of equal diameter mounted parallel to one another on a common spindle, came as early as 1866, although no such design became widely available until several years later when the "Welch" and the "Otto" appeared. The Otto was patented by Edward Carl Friedrich Otto in 1879–1881, manufactured by the B.S.A. Company and marketed through the Otto Bicycle Company, London. This elegant machine had a saddle and pedal cranks from which the effort of the rider was transmitted by means of pulleys and belts to the two large driving-wheels. Steering was achieved by slackening one of these belts so that one wheel rotated faster than the other, thus causing the machine to turn.

Above: *John Player cigarette card showing a Salvo Tricycle being ridden by James Starley. Queen Victoria bought two Salvo Tricycles in 1881.*

Above left: *Coventry Rotary Tricycle.*

Below left: *Centaur Tandem Tricycle, c. 1884.*

The Salvoquadricycle was driven by two large wheels, and steered by a small front wheel with a rack-and-pinion system. A hand brake was applied by means of a lever. The balance gear distributed the power evenly to both wheels through the incorporation of a bevel-gear differential unit in the axle to equalize the drive.

Orders for the Salvo flooded in and agents were appointed all over the country. By 1878, Starley's factory in Coventry had produced more than 100 of these machines. The 1879 catalogue for the Salvoquadricycle describes it as: "Not for an age, but for all time", and "Unequalled for ease, speed, grace and safety".

Starley's also produced a ladies' light-

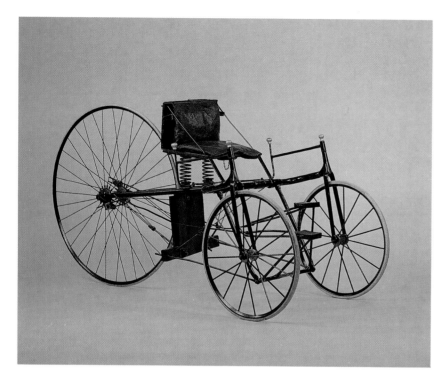

Above: *Dublin Tricycle, c. 1876.*

Right: *The Excelsior Tricycle.*

The Otto had many enthusiastic riders, both male and female, who declared that their aesthetic mounts were for the artistic rather than for the racing public. In fact, no races were open to Ottos but this did not stop individual riders from trying out their machines on the circuits and over long-distance rides.

However, the tricycles remained the more popular design and after an initially tentative period of production they increased in popularity. By the close of 1879 there were some twenty varieties of tricycle manufactured in Coventry alone.

Whereas the Ordinary in the early 1880s changed little, the tricycle underwent constant modifications as a result of technical improvements and subtle experimentation until it became quite sophisticated in design. Continual discussions and blatant arguments raged regarding these experiments and improvements. For example, should the steering system be in front, at the side or at the rear? Should steering be direct or indirect? Is front-drive, side-drive or rear-drive more efficient? Should the seating be sociable, solo or tandem? (One of the first double tricycle designs was the Coventry dos-a-dos, manufactured in around 1879. This machine was a Coventry Lever Tricycle with a second set of levers behind, and the

Below right: *A cartoon from Punch, 18 February 1914, "Oh, Jockywock darling, you must try and remember it's a tricycle not a bicycle."*

"OH, JOCKYWOCK DARLING, YOU *MUST* TRY AND REMEMBER IT'S A TRICYCLE, NOT A BICYCLE."

two riders sat back to back). Eventually, the arguments were settled in favour of front-steering and handlebars replaced the rack-and-pinion.

The mid-1880s represented a period of immense charm. There were no other vehicles on the road to rival bicycles and tricycles for economy. The Bicycle Touring Club had a chain of friendly hotels and restaurants where riders could eat and drink for a fixed tariff. Clubs attracted many new members. The neat, uniformed clubman would be seen in the black silk cricket cap he wore for general use, or possibly in a straw hat for warmer weather. The ladies would ride in their Norfolk-type jackets, plain skirts and soft Alpine hats or even in a coat bodice, skirt with panniers and apron, and a straw hat. Special helmets could be worn by both men and women. However there were still complaints that skirts were too short and many objections were raised concerning the sight of ladies' shoes, or worse still the indecorous display of lower leg that might occur in a slight breeze. Towards the 1890s women's tight jackets began to puff at the sleeves and the elegant "leg of mutton" design came to the forefront of ladies' cycling costume.

The Sociable tricycle gave women the chance to ride out with their husbands even though their flowing, cumbersome outfits were still hardly ideal for this type of exercise. Cycling was now becoming a family affair, with groups of both sexes and all ages enjoying the freedom and exercise associated with independent mobility. Touring was immensely popular. English people began to travel round Europe on tricycles, and even women were able to assert their independence by this means. However, some still saw this as a lowering of standards, especially when women and men were seen Sociable-riding together.

The teething period, in general, was over and most people had grown used to the new machines and were prepared to allow them to share the public highways. However, the picture had not always been so rosy, much of the early antagonism coming from the tricyclists, who considered bicyclists an inferior breed. The tricycle, its riders argued, was comfortable, unstrenuous, relaxing and more practical, since it could be ridden over

stones without dismounting so that the tricyclists themselves were more dignified because they did not have to degrade themselves by constantly hopping off and remounting their steeds.

In 1880 there was a strong feeling that tricyclists should break away from the Bicycle Touring Club and form their own central organization, and in 1882 the Tricycle Union was formed.

Immediately there were fresh arguments about uniform. Each sport of this period had its own costume, so why should not tricycle-riding? Or so asserted an opinionated editorial in *The Tricyclist* of 1882. Discussions then raged, as they did for bicyclists, regarding correct dress. Knee breeches, for example, should fit but not too close and jackets should lay close without being too tight.

Tricycles and Sociables took up huge amounts of space to store. One solution was a tandem tricycle, on which the riders sat one behind the other, and as this machine improved the Sociable tricycle eventually disappeared.

The middle years of the 1880s produced an outburst of activity in the development of tricycles and bicycles alike. Dwarf Safeties were appearing and although the Ordinary was declining in popularity there was still a wide variety of models on the market.

The Singer Tricycle, c. 1888.

A cyclometer made by the Pope Manufacturing Company, Boston. It is a waterproof can, with a glass face, which is attached to the axle inside the front wheel, and revolves with the wheel.

Above: *Photograph of Ordinary riding in club uniform.*

Right: *Photograph of Mr G.L. Lacy Hillier with his bicycle. Mr Lacy Hillier was founder of the Cyclists' Union.*

Top: Tandem tricycle made by the Coventry Machinsts' Company.

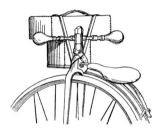

Above: Harvard Handle-bag.

Left: An advertisement for cycling accessories, 1899.

At the 1883 Stanley Show there were 289 tricycles as opposed to 233 bicycles, an imbalance which continued well into 1888, when there were still more tricycles than bicycles at the annual shows. To begin with, no one design gained wider acceptance than any other, and each manufacturer continued to proclaim superiority for his own type. Then after 1885 the type of tricycle design to find favour was one with a loop frame, a side or a central gear, and a single central backbone.

An important example of the central gear type was the Humber. During the early 1880s, the Humber was much faster than any other machine. This simple yet practical model had two large driving-wheels, connected by a balance-geared axle, backbone and rear trailing wheel. It weighed around 100 lb. This design was at first preferred by many tricyclists, especially since it did well on the track and proved easier to ride on hills. Riding such a model, Lacy Hillier won the 50-mile road championships in 1881, in a time of 4 hours 53 minutes.

With increased speeds, tricycles attracted riders who were both athletic and competitive. Clubs for both sexes were booming and in 1882 *The Tricyclist* magazine was first published.

Amateur championships excited a great deal of interest and drew large crowds,

usually a battalion of inquisitive bicyclists. Ladies had their own class of races. Since it was now quite common to see ladies riding, however, little comment was passed.

In 1882 Starley's Coventry Rotary Tricycle, with a central chain-drive, won the annual 50-mile road championship in 3 hours 47 minutes 40 seconds. The machine weighed only 48½ lb. and was ridden by Lowndes. On 7 July 1883, the London Tricycle Club held a 24-hour open race. There were 67 competitors and the event was won by T.R. Marriot, captain of the London Tricycle Club, who achieved 218¾ miles.

In 1886 a new design of tricycle was introduced which constantly won such races, and by 1887 the Humber Cripper had become so popular, particularly for towing and for ladies that it made many other models redundant. Named after a well-known rider called R. Cripps, from Nottingham, who achieved a great deal of success on this type of tricycle, the Humber Cripper was one of those designed with a single central backbone and a central gear, though this machine incorporated a 20-inch diameter front steering-wheel which was held in a long, inclined steering column.

The Cripper replaced the earlier design of Humber tricycle and over the years that followed the model was further improved by increasing the size of the front wheel and reducing the weight of the frame. The side differential gear box successfully supported the axle in four places. Eventually, the design evolved into a direct steering machine and later still it developed into the modern design of tricycle, one of the earliest versions of which was the "Singer" of 1888.

The Starley Brothers introduced their own design similar to the Humber Cripper. This was called the "Psycho". The firm of Starley Brothers, founded around 1875, began manufacture in Fleet Street, Coventry. After the death of James Starley, his three sons, James, John and William carried on the business. In 1884 Starley Brothers moved to St John's works and James Starley left the business. In 1896 the firm was sold and amalgamated with Westwood Company, as Starley Brothers & Westwood Manufacturing Company Limited.

The Psycho tricycle was made by Starley Brothers in about 1886. Weighing around

Postman on a tricycle in Vienna, 1888.

Above: *A Milk Delivery Tricycle.*

Below left: *Wall's Ice Cream Tricycle.*

Below: *John Player cigarette card showing the notable tricyclist F.T. Bidlake.*

*B*read Delivery Tricycle,
1920s.

*J*ohn Player cigarette card
showing an Invincible
Tandem Tricycle. This was a
rear-steering machine.

76½ lb. it was fitted with John Starley's automatic steering device, which was concealed in the main frame tube behind the steering-head. This kept the small steering-wheel in a straight line, and automatically returned it to this line after it had been turned by the handlebar.

The Starley Brothers also manufactured a tandem Psycho. Described as essentially a touring machine, it attracted good reviews. The design allowed a large amount of room between the two riders, "who may consist of ladies or gentlemen indiscriminately", as an advertisement stated in February 1887. Steering was of the "fashionable" handlebar kind and was under control of the front rider. A tandem version of the Humber Cripper too was produced by adding a second seat behind the normal one and providing a second set of pedals, with chain-drive to the differential gear on the axle.

Tandem tricycles were raced as well. In the first race organized by North Road Cycling Club in 1886 A.J. Wilson and C.E. Liles beat all the competition, which included Ordinaries, Safeties and Solo tricyclists. This led to tandem tricycles being handicapped, a practice that continued until improvements in the rear-driven Safety gave it increased speed and popularity.

In 1928, George Humber Spencer formed an institution devoted solely to the tricycle and the promotion of tricycle racing. The Tricycle Association was created because tricycles were banned from certain competitions and, therefore, required their own organization and events. The association survived the war years with a depleted membership, and in 1950 a women's group was set up by Mrs D. Tuffnell. This was developed because women were still not allowed to amalgamate with the association proper. Today, the Tricycle Association has about 600 members nationwide and the eight regions manage separate races, charity rides and record-breaking attempts. All manner of tricycles are seen at meetings, including invalid tricycles and recumbent tricycles.

The tricycle was never especially popular in the United States of America. It enjoyed a short burst of success in 1887 when the praises of the "Quadrant" were sung because, it was claimed, American roads were so dreadful that only this tricycle, rather than the Cripper type, would stand them. The Quadrant was patented in 1882, and was a rear-driven and rear-steered tricycle. This design introduced the large diameter steering-wheel to replace the small diameter wheel. A later Quadrant design which appeared in 1884 was front-steering and also employed handlebar control.

During the course of its development, the tricycle was used for commercial purposes as well as for touring and racing. Having proved an efficient alternative means of passenger transport to the horse, the cycle was also adapted to carry goods and the three-wheeled designs performed best. After the diamond frame was established most manufacturers had a workhorse model in their stables. Mainly black in colour, they were not trend-setters but standard functional machines.

As early as 1881 Bayliss and Thomas obtained the first contract for the supply of carrier tricycles to the Post Office, and before long this design was being used by various trades and for deliveries of a wide range of goods. Carriers encouraged prosperity in many businesses, with errand boys delivering orders door to door. The Post Office still holds dear to its faithful carrier cycle, even though the advent of cars and supermarkets has caused the demise of the errand boy. "Pashley" still produce in large numbers for Post Office needs.

During the latter years of the 1880s greater refinements were introduced in tricycle design. Driving-wheels were shrinking to as little as 30 inches, saddles were improved, vibration had to be overcome, gearing perfected and in 1889 the pneumatic tyre began to make its presence felt. About a dozen firms fitted pneumatics to some of their machines at the 1890 Stanley Show.

However, for all these refinements the lever-driven model still had its devotees — especially amongst women who appreciated the absence of a dirty chain in which skirts could be caught. Besides, it was somehow more dignified to ride with a stately up-and-down motion than in a rotary one.

The 1890s saw a decline in the appeal of the tricycle, as attention turned chiefly to the production of the Safety bicycle. The main disadvantage of the tricycle was its weight. In 1886, for example, the lightest racing tricycles weighed between 40 and 45 lb., roadsters up to 60 lb. and many Soci-

ables even more. Because of this weight, the tricycle was more difficult to propel, particularly uphill or against a wind. It also required more storage room than the lighter and more practical Safety bicycle.

Yet the tricycle has remained popular even up to the present day, especially for children. Smaller, cheaper tricycles for young people were first available in about 1870, and many children still learn to ride and experience for the first time the excitement of independent mobility on the saddle of a tricycle.

Above: *The Pashley Post Office Cycle.*

Below: *Trade Cycle.*

A Transitional
Period

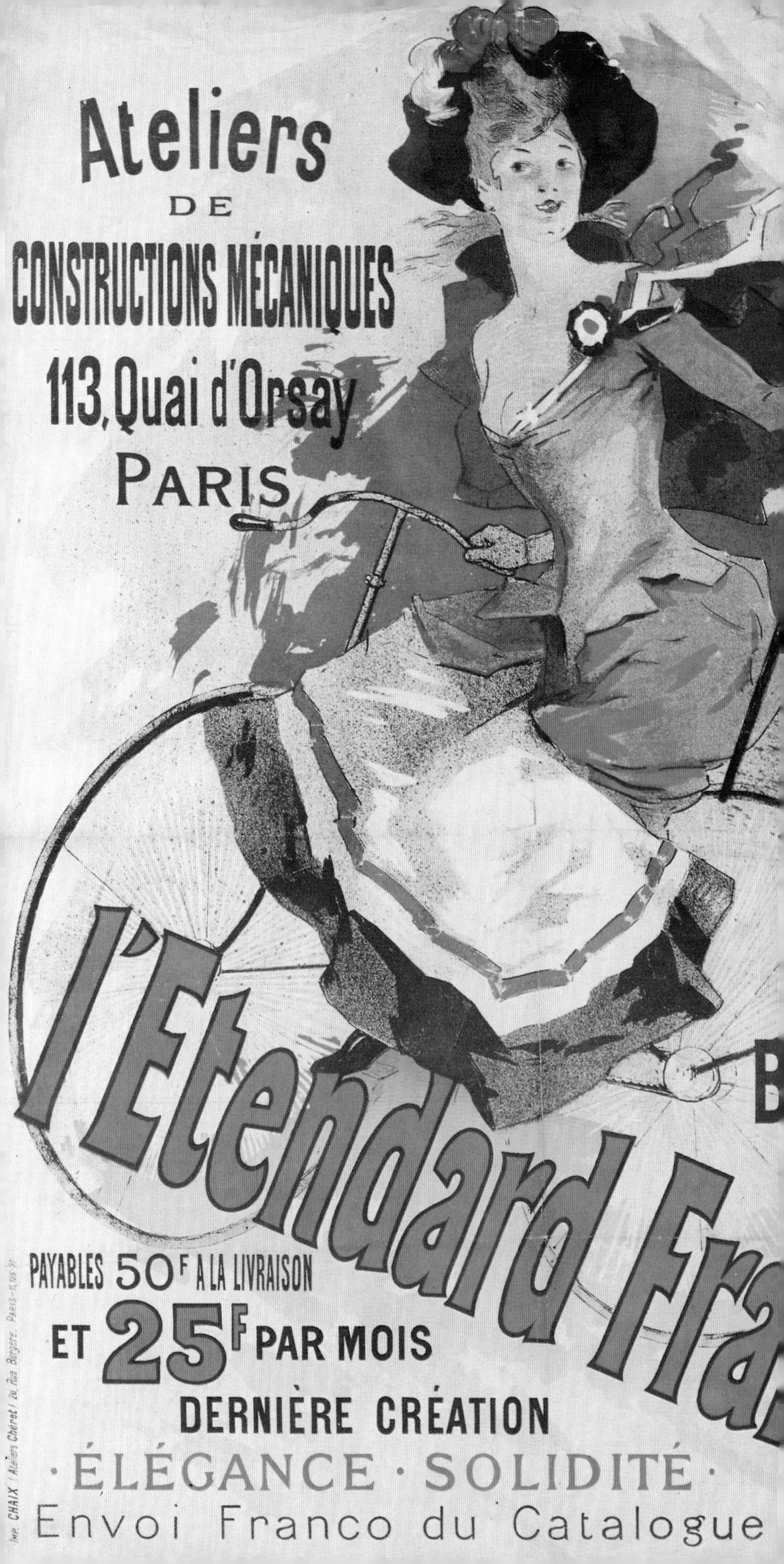
Ateliers
DE
CONSTRUCTIONS MÉCANIQUES
113, Quai d'Orsay
PARIS
l'Etendard Fra
B
PAYABLES 50F A LA LIVRAISON
ET 25F PAR MOIS
DERNIÈRE CRÉATION
·ÉLÉGANCE·SOLIDITÉ·
Envoi Franco du Catalogue
IMP. CHAIX (Ateliers Chéret) 20, Rue Bergère. PARIS

A TRANSITIONAL PERIOD:
INCLUDING DWARFS

During the period of the Ordinary there were many attempts to popularize Safety cycles, that is to say, geared-up, rear-driven machines. All through the period of tricycle domination the search for a Safety machine continued quietly in the background until the market was ready for the improved design. Once the demand was there, however, the Safety was an almost overnight success and sales of alternative mounts rapidly declined.

The Safety design evolved gradually. Various attempts had been made from 1869 onwards to produce a bicycle that was safer to ride. The first to meet with any success were driven by levers as opposed to pedal cranks attached directly to the centre of the front wheel. Of these, two of the more successful designs produced were called the "Facile" and the "Xtraordinary".

The Facile was invented by John Beale and was patented in 1878. For the first three years the machines were sold privately, until manufacturers Messrs Ellis & Co., London, introduced the new model to the public at the fourth Stanley Show.

Often described as the first notable machine of the Safety class, the Facile's safer riding position (that is, the greater distance of the rider behind the front forks) made it a great improvement for elderly riders. The popular cycling press of the period approved it, asserting that it increased the number of those who cycled. An 1885 advertisement for the Facile indicates the range of riders at whom the machine was aimed: " . . . among these are not a few over 60 years of age and several over 70, the 'Facile' being equally suitable for the elderly as for the young and athletic rider".

The Facile was a frequent topic of correspondence between cyclists. In January 1888 a J.E. Keates wrote in the *Cyclists' Touring Club Gazette*: "I brought a 42" Facile over six years since . . . and have ridden it each year some thousands of miles with much pleasure. I am over 70 years of age, and there is not a mark or scratch on my person arising from riding." As might be expected, however, not all cyclists took to the machine with equal enthusiasm. In the same edition of the *CTC Gazette* "TIFOS" writes: "I should be very sorry to recommend the facile as a 'Safety' bicycle for it has an ugly trick of 'Tipping up' when going downhill, and I have come many 'a cropper' over the handlebars."

The design of the Facile was such that the pedals were lowered by pivoting them on the ends of levers which were mounted below the front wheel hub. These levers pivoted at the front ends to lower the extensions of the front forks and the midpoints were connected to cranks by short articulated links. The machine weighed only 32 lb.

A Facile club flourished in South London and races for Facile-riders only were organized by the manufacturers Ellis & Co. In 1882, W. Snook of Winchester won the first Facile 24-hours road race, covering 214½ miles on a machine with a 42-inch front wheel. The race was repeated in 1883 and won this time by Joseph Harris Adams, who covered a total of 221¼ miles. In 1884 Adams beat the Land's End to John o'Groats record on a Facile, with a time inside seven days.

The "Xtraordinary" was made by Singer & Co. Limited, Coventry, and was patented by George Singer in 1878. Singer was born

Opposite: *Advertising poster by Jules Chéret. 'The first printing machines able to turn out large quantities of posters in colour were perfected in the 1870s – just as the Ordinary cycle, or Penny Farthing, was making its debut. The boom in bicycle sales that followed later led to posters being extensively used for cycle advertising.' Mumbles Railway Company Ltd.*

Facile Dwarf Safety Roadster.

*K*angaroo, c. 1884.

*T*he 'Singer' of 1889.

*R*ight: *A Dutch advertisement for the Kangaroo Safety Bicycle.*

in Sussex in 1847 and died in Coventry in 1909. In 1868 he was a foreman in the works of the Coventry Sewing Machine Company, but left there in 1875 to start his own business.

Designed for safety rather than speed, the Xtraordinary soon became a great favourite and achieved large sales for several years. Correspondence about it was again lively amongst the cyclists. Letters for and against the Xtraordinary appeared in each new edition of the *CTC Gazette*, with its supporters coming well out on top. In August 1886 H.A. Allbutt wrote in the *Gazette*: "I have ridden over 2,000 miles, and have not spent a single penny in repairs. I know no better or more comfortable bicycle for all-round work and touring purposes than an . . . 'Xtra'. I have long since come to the conclusion never to ride any other bicycle."

Like the Facile the Xtraordinary also used levers, but the pivot point was placed just below the handlebars. Crank pins were joined to the levers which moved in an arc. The front forks were raked forwards from the steering-head and this placed the saddle further back, adding to the safety of the machine. A feature of the Xtraordinary was its rubber-studded pedals.

During this period French and American machines came to be fairly well known in Britain. Publications were full of diagrams

and engineering formulae, and the cycle shows were a happy hunting ground for enthusiasts seeking information about all kinds of international inventions.

In 1885 Gormully & Teffeny of Chicago patented an American Safety designed with lever propulsion. The driving-wheel was 46 inches and the hind wheel 20 inches and the total weight of the machine was 43 lb. This Safety was described in an advertisement of the period as follows: "Strongly built and well suited for use in country around Chicago and America generally".

The American lever gear used in this machine was arranged with the intention of driving a small wheel. The swinging rods were slightly shorter and the pedal ends of the levers were bent downwards. The joints in the swinging rods were on the ball-and-socket principle.

As early as 1877, a Frenchman named Rousseau invented a geared-up chain-drive Safety bicycle, but his machine did not catch on in France at that time, and it was not until 1884 that any model using the principle behind this design appeared in England. This machine was called the "Kangaroo".

Introduced by Hillman, Herbert & Cooper at the Stanley Show, Covent Garden, the Kangaroo was an early example of a Dwarf front-driving Safety bicycle.

Hillman, Herbert & Cooper started in business in 1876. Of the three partners, William Hillman had previously been a foreman at the Coventry Sewing Machine Company. A practical mechanic, he died in 1921. William Henry Herbert came from

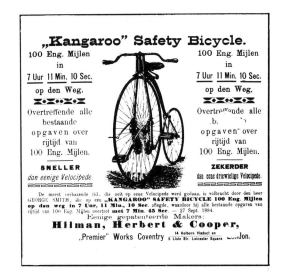

Leicester, and it was he who dealt with the financial side of the business, whereas George Beverley Cooper handled the commercial side. Cooper managed the company's London depot and when the firm was floated as the Premier Cycle Company he left. He died in 1919.

The Kangaroo incorporated a chain-drive to the hub, a feature which came to be widely copied by many manufacturers. The design also established the principle of gearing up a bicycle by fitting different-sized sprockets. Thus, with one revolution of the crank the driving-wheel could travel further than the driving-wheel of an Ordinary. Many of the additional improvements, such as the use of ball bearings, spring saddles and spoon brakes, were patented by Hillman in 1884. The design also introduced larger cranks of approximately 7 inches.

The Kangaroo rage lasted only two seasons. This design and its many copies leapt into the forefront of fashion largely because it was safer and easier to mount and dismount than an Ordinary. The *Cyclists' Touring Club Gazette* of November 1884 published an editorial on the Kangaroo and described it as a: " . . . sound and reliable little mount, likely to win its way more and more into popular favour, particularly among those who value their necks too highly to risk them upon the Ordinary bicycle . . . ".

During 1884 there were few first-class manufacturers who did not make a machine of a similar type. Club runs on the design were popular and, according to *The Cyclist* magazine, some were in the form of Kangaroo Hunts, a game of hare and hounds on wheels with the Kangaroo having a four-minute start. Described as "The only true Safety" in an 1885 advertisement, the Kangaroo inevitably had enormous appeal. As the manufacturers claimed, not only was it "safer than a tricycle" and "Faster than a bicycle", but they also claimed "over 100 of these machines selling weekly".

Apart from considerations of safety, another reason for the new bicycle's popularity was the number of record-breaking times and distances being achieved which could never have been contemplated on the Ordinary. These records on both path and road offered proof of its superiority in speed

over any machine previously introduced.

However, the majority of die-hard Ordinary riders, many of whom were C.T.C. members, still refused to accept the new designs and treated them with narrow-minded scorn. One of these, member No. 20,885 wrote in the December 1887 issue of the *Gazette* comparing the Ordinary to a Facile: "The rotary motion of an Ordinary is infinitely to be preferred to the wearying up and down of the Facile". And he concludes "the only recommendation of the Facile is

Above: *Geared Facile, c. 1885.*

Below: *Cross-frame Safety Cycle, 1890.*

A Training Cycle, c. 1875.

that, in case of a fall, one does not have so far to go."

Yet, there were some cyclists who could see the limitations of the Ordinary, such as its fixed gear ratio and its sheer size. In February 1888 "G.H.P." wrote a letter in the *CTC Gazette* entitled "Ordinary versus safety": "Sir, I am quite aware that a bicyclette is safer, and its saddle more easy of access". These problems had to be over-

come, and the solution eventually came in the form of a geared Ordinary, which actually extended the life of a dying breed.

The gear of an Ordinary was quite simply the circumference of the large wheel. A taller rider could bestride a higher wheel and therefore have a larger gear. The geared Ordinary allowed a smaller front driving-wheel to be used and thus reduced the overall size of the machine. The gear ratio could be adjusted by the addition of a gear-train, which enabled the driving-wheel to be turned more quickly. Pedals were placed at a lower level than had been the case when they were connected directly to the hub and this meant that the rider sat further back from the steering-head.

The popularity of the Dwarf Safeties had diminished the appeal of the Facile, and so it was not long before Ellis & Co. London produced a geared Facile to meet the growing demands voiced by cyclists. This machine made its appearance at the 1887 Autumn Stanley Show.

The geared Facile combined lever-drive with sun-and-planet gearing, described as the simplest mechanical motion on the market during this period. The action of the gear was direct, straight and powerful. A large-toothed wheel (the sun) was fitted to

the axle. The crank extended an inch or so beyond the edge of this wheel. At the crank end a second crank was fitted, revolving in a bearing and carrying on the other side a small-toothed wheel (the planet) which geared in the larger one. The pressure upon the pedal placed at the end of this secondary crank drew the large wheel round and in the course of its travels the wheel was geared up to the extent of the added diameter of the smaller wheel, with each wheel making one revolution. In this way a 40-inch Facile could be geared up to 60 inches.

The front forks of the geared Facile were raked forward, so that the rider was positioned further behind the centre of the front wheel. Weighing only 37 lb., this machine was used to set several new records, especially when fitted with pneumatic tyres. In 1888 297 miles were covered on it in 24 hours, and in 1890 the London to Brighton run was completed in 7 hours 50 minutes.

In 1892 a geared Ordinary was introduced by the Crypto Cycle Co. Ltd, London. This machine employed a spindle which carried a pinion. The inner circumference of the hub incorporated a ring of teeth. Between the teeth and the pinion was a set of three small pinions revolving on studs affixed to the hub-flange. By such means a 49-inch driving-wheel was geared up to about 62 inches. The Crypto Alpha Bantam, made by the Crypto Cycle Co. Ltd, marked the last of the attempts to maintain the popularity of front driving as against chain-drive to the rear wheel.

During the transitional period between Ordinary and Safety bicycles many new models came and went, some in response to the dictates of fashion, some as innovatory attempts to meet cyclists' demands for greater speed, stability, ease, comfort, or indeed for whatever happened to be the concern of the time. Thus, the tricycle gained ground at the expense of the Ordinary; from 1886 to 1888 there were more tricycles than bicycles at the annual shows. Then, when Dwarfs were manufactured in great numbers, the tricycle in its turn fell into decline. Eventually, when gearing was added to the Ordinary the development of the diamond frame had already begun and the geared Ordinary was overtaken by the production of the Rover Safety.

Left: *Cycles used by acrobats.*

Bottom left: *The cycle sports arena in Paris, 1893.*

Below: *John Player cigarette card of an Olympia Tandem Tricycle. In 1890, Mr Bates and Mr Edge, the riders of this machine, rode a distance of 100 miles in 5½ hours.*

EARLY SAFETY BICYCLES: INCLUDING
SPRING FRAMES AND PNEUMATICS

The late 1880s witnessed another period of experimentation, although this time the impetus was towards a rear-driven Safety bicycle, for once manufacturers and inventors alike finally believed in the superiority of this design all alternatives were abandoned. A variety of models continued to be ridden at this time, including tricycles, Ordinaries, and Dwarfs, all of which were bidding for acceptance as the best model. But even before the Edwardian period both consumers and producers had rejected these as novelties and had opted for the design that has survived to this day – the diamond-frame Safety bicycle.

The fact that the new machines were described as "Safety" cycles underlines the precarious nature of many of their predecessors, and of the Ordinary in particular. A "Safe" model offered the increased stability to be found on two wheels which are the same size, although some early Safeties had a front wheel which was slightly smaller than the hind wheel, and thus a lower centre of gravity.

Experimental designs appeared in the early 1870s. In 1873/4 H.J. Lawson created what is now reputed to be the first authentic and practical design of a Safety bicycle which employed a chain-drive to the hind wheel. Henry Lawson was born in London on 23 February 1852. A mechanically minded man, he began his career within the cycle trade in Brighton. Eventually he moved from Brighton to Coventry where he became manager of the Tangent and Coventry Tricycle Company.

The prototype bicycle invented by Lawson employed a lever system which drove the hind wheel by means of connecting rods.

Affectionately called the "Crocodile", its final design was patented in 1876. Marketed by Singer & Company, the Crocodile was only on sale for a very short period. This did not, however, deter Lawson's fertile experimental mind and he began to explore the idea of a chain-driven Safety. Various designs followed until the "Bicyclette" was patented in 1879. A much improved version of the Safety, the Bicyclette was manufactured by the Rudge Company and provoked considerable comment at the Stanley Show of 1880. It was a chain-driven Safety, with the chain-drive taken via a chain wheel to the hub of the hind wheel. It had a 40-inch front wheel, a 24-inch hind wheel and raked front forks.

Opposite: The Pretty Cyclist and the perils of the road, 1896.

The Otto Patent Safety Bicycle, c. 1882.

Although his basic idea was sound, Lawson found that the frame was not rigid enough and improvements were therefore needed. The Bicyclette appears not to have been very popular, perhaps because it was marketed too early.

During the next ten years or so the experiments continued with a variety of diverse designs, all marking an important step in the evolution of the modern rear-driven bicycle. Thomas Sherigold, a Gloucester shoemaker, for example, produced a chain-driven Safety during this period, although he unfortunately lacked the means to develop it. On the Continent, also, new developments were taking shape. In 1877, Rousseau of Marseilles constructed a Safety which employed its chain-drive to the front wheel.

By the 1880s there was a great influx of such innovative designs. Manufacturers such as Humber, B.S.A. and McCammon, to name just three, had each produced a Safety bicycle. The McCammon was notable for its use of a single-tube drop frame which made it suitable for use by women. However, it was the great name of Starley, which, in 1885, established the Safety bicycle commercially by producing the highly successful and influential "Rover".

John Kemp Starley (1854–1901) was the son of James Starley's elder brother John. In 1871 he worked as a mechanic at Haynes and Jeffries' Ariel works until 1877–1878 when he began his own business. He was later joined by William Sutton, and together they formed Starley & Sutton of the Meteor Works, West Orchard, Coventry. After trying various experimental designs Starley exhibited his improved Rover at the 1885 Stanley Show, and with it established the superiority of the rear-wheel chain-driven bicycle. Exported to America, France, Germany, Italy, Austria, Switzerland, Australia and India, amongst other places, the Rover heralded a great expansion in the bicycle trade and was speedily copied by many manufacturers.

During the early years of the Rover,

The 'Rover' made by J.K. Starley, 1885.

A photograph of Dan Albone – a Thorough Good Fellow 1860–1906; inventor of cycles, motor cars, the first practical farm tractor and the father of the British tractor industry.

Early models had seen substantial modifications, especially to the rear steering arrangement. Some changes had been suggested by Stephen Golder, a Coventry Competition Cyclist.

The year 1885 was the right time to market the Rover. An advertisement in that year asked, "Have you seen the Rover safety?" then goes on to say, "If not, do so at once — and try it". The public did try it and with great enthusiasm, although many Ordinary riders still proved obstinate and refused to be swayed without a battle, and a battle they got, not only on the leisure trail but also on the race track.

Another 1885 advertisement for the Rover states "Pronounced by experts as the FASTEST cycle ever made. One trial will prove this". On 26 September 1885 the Rover was raced by George Smith, who duly set a new 100-mile record of 7 hours, 5 minutes and 16 seconds. For many people this confirmed the superiority of a model with chain-drive to back wheel over the front-drive Ordinary. Alternative and popular mounts for racing were the cross-frame Safeties. Many records were broken by such machines; however, they lacked the strength of the diamond-frame Rover.

One of the more popular cross-frame Safeties was the "Ivel" made by Dan Albone and named after the river which ran through his home town. Born in the village of Biggleswade, Bedfordshire, in 1860, Albone was a self-taught mechanic who in 1886 produced a cross-frame Safety racing bicycle. Weighing only 27½ lb., the Ivel was made in comparatively small numbers, yet it secured a substantial reputation among racing cyclists. Part of the success of the model may have been due to Dan's personality. Formerly of the Ongley Arms Hotel, later the Ivel Hotel, behind which his workshops

Above left: Crypto – Bantam, c. 1894.

Below left: The McCammon Safety Bicycle, 1884.

commentators boldly stated that finally a machine had been produced which fully deserved the name "Safety". They went on to list its assets, including reduced vibration, easier steering, the advantages of a narrow tread and a single chain, its improved luggage-carrying and its speed.

The principal feature of the Rover was the backbone frame. A curved seat tube, which brought the rear wheel closer to the bracket, bisected this backbone and continued down to form a housing for the crank axle. The bottom bracket was connected to the rear of the frame by chain-stays. Although the chain gathered dirt and could stretch, the Rover had a unique and simple method of adjustment, since the back wheel could be moved backwards or forwards as required.

Left: The Safety Bicycle (Messrs. Hillman, Herbert and Cooper).

Below: *The Ivel Tandem, 1888.*

Bottom: *Linley & Biggs 'Whippet' Safety Bicycle, 1888.*

were located, Albone was a popular figure among the cycling fraternity and a champion cyclist in his own right. He had won the district championship on five occasions and had several times held the county championship. In addition to racing, inventing, and running the hotel, Albone also ran the local cycling club and helped riders in pursuit of record honours or time trials. *Cycling* magazine of 2 May 1891 said of Dan Albone: "There is not a man of record-breaking intent to whom he has not rendered some valuable assistance . . . ". The article continued: "He is a sportsman above all things:

on the road Dan Albone is best known as an ever willing pacemaker, but on the race path he has won a big sheaf of awards . . . ".

The year 1886 saw the design and construction of the first practical tandem. The "Ivel Tandem" was produced by Dan Albone with A.J. Wilson, but it was not commercially manufactured until about 1888. Built on the cross-frame principle, it had a single diagonal backbone whose low riding position made it suitable for ladies as well as gentlemen. The handlebars were coupled so the machine could be steered by either rider. However, the coupling of both handlebars was discontinued when it was realised how impractical it was, and in 1888 Albone and E.J. Willis rode 20 miles on the Paddington Track in 1 hour, 5 minutes and 55⅘ seconds on an improved model.

Albone may also have been responsible for the first practical ladies' Safety bicycle. The model was developed from his cross-frame design by replacing the straight front tube with a curved tube from the steering-head to the pedal bracket. In addition, this bicycle incorporated a leather dress-guard which was laced onto the frame secured to the chain-stays over the rear wheel. At the close of Albone's life he went on to manufacture motorcycles and cars as well as bicycles. He died in 1906.

During this fertile period the diamond frame continued to develop and with its advent other designs fell out of favour. However, there were still many problems to overcome, and experiments to refine the bicycle carried on, particularly with regard to such areas as the transmission. One solution was the shaft drive with bevel gears. As far back as 1882 such a device had been applied to tricycle propulsion and by the 1890s it was incorporated into bicycles such as the "Quadrant" (1898), which weighed 35¼ lb. Later designs using shaft drive included the Belgian "F.N."; however these bicycles made little headway against the now established roller chain-drive and as a result were little used.

The design of the Whippet bicycle was such that the wheels were connected to each other by a rigid frame, which pivoted on the back wheel axle and carried the handlebars, saddle and pedals, which were all built on a rigid triangle and suspended from the wheel-

ers were obliged to retool existing models with forks wide enough to take the new tyres. Soon scarcely any new bicycles or tricycles were to be found with solid tyres. The pneumatic tyre had to come to stay, and with its arrival areas of the country that previously had been difficult to ride in, or positively inaccessible, were opened up to cyclists, who could ride through or tour around them with a fair degree of comfort.

The popularity of racing also increased to an enormous extent with the introduction of the pneumatic tyre. As early as 1889 a cyclist named W. Hume entered a race at Queens College Sports Ground in Belfast on a bicycle with Dunlop tyres. In all four heats that he entered, Hume easily beat the cyclists

Left: John Boyd Dunlop, 1840–1921. Founder of the pneumatic tyre industry. On 23 July 1888, he patented his invention giving these few details: 'Chamber made of rubber or any other material suitable for holding air under pressure or otherwise, affixed to the wheel by the most advantageous method'.

Below: An advertisement for the Whippet cycle from the Illustrated London News, 21 July 1888.

Bottom: Dunlop's son on the first bicycle to have pneumatic tyres.

frame by a spring. This spring allowed the wheels to roll over obstacles without affecting the position of the rider. The Whippet bicycle weighed 43½ lb. and was used for record-breaking with some success.

Similar efforts to reduce vibration resulted in the manufacture of alternative spring frames, telescopic seat rods and handlebar tubes containing coiled springs. However, such designs became redundant with the advent of a special innovation which came as a breath of fresh air to both bicycle manufacturers and consumers.

John Boyd Dunlop was born in Dreghorn, south-western Scotland, in 1840. He subsequently moved to Ireland, where he became a veterinary surgeon in Belfast. Dunlop was an intelligent man with a problem-solving mind; so much so, that when asked by his son to make a tricycle run faster and with great comfort, he set about experimenting with rubber tubing, rubbered canvas and inflation with air. Thus, in 1888, the pneumatic tyre was invented.

An original Dublin firm, the Pneumatic Tyre and Booth's Cycle Agency Limited, established in 1889, moved to Coventry in 1892 and became the Dunlop Pneumatic Tyre Company. Finally, in 1900, the company moved to Birmingham, and was named the Dunlop Rubber Company Limited.

By 1892 pneumatic tyres were established as being essential for speed and comfort, whether touring or racing, and manufactur-

Right: *Oil lamps: Powell & Hamner 'Horoscope' and Lucas 'New Holophote' and candle lamps.*

Middle: *Acetylene lamps: 'King of the Road' and 'Aceta' and carbide tins.*

Below right: *Dynohub, electric and battery lamps.*

Below: *John Player cigarette card of the Novel Tandem of the '90s. Although the lady always sat in front, the man did the steering from behind.*

who were racing on solid tyres.

As faster times were achieved upon the track, it became necessary to improve the tracks themselves and the outside banks became higher and higher. Pacing also became better, until purely pacing teams were being used.

Following the initial introduction of the pneumatic tyre, further innovations occurred in the tyre industry in an effort to improve on the original design. In 1896, for example, an American called H.J. Doughty invented a steam-heated press for the vulcanization of bicycle tyres. This opened the way to mass production of bicycle tyres with complex patterns in their tread.

The pneumatic tyre was also developed abroad, in particular by the brothers André and Edouard Michelin in France. In 1892, two patents were taken out by the Michelin Company for bead-edged tyres, which were secured in position on the wheel-rims by means of rings. The French were quick to recognize the importance of pneumatic tyres, particularly after Jiel Laval achieved an easy win over the then champion, Terront, in the Paris to Brest road race on a bicycle fitted with the new tyres. With the extraordinary demand for their tyres a licence had been obtained from the Dunlop parent company for exclusive manufacture in Levallois, Perret, in France within three

years of the tyre's introduction. The company was named the Compagnie Francaise des Pneumatics Dunlop. During the 1890s cycling increased in popularity in France to become the premier outdoor amusement. The seat of the cycle trade was in Paris and with lesser centres in Angers, Dijon, Lyon and St Etienne.

Over the last years of the nineteenth century the diamond-frame design had become standard although a variety of alternative models continued to be produced during the early 1890s. Among these the "Singer" had a single curved tube for the saddle support. The first modern form of diamond-frame bicycle to go into production was the "Humber", in which the frame had a slightly sloping top tube. This tilted downwards on the racing model to give a lower handlebar position. With wheels of almost equal diameter, the Humber employed chain-drive to the rear wheel, and a spring-saddle on an adjustable saddle tube.

Many manufacturers now adopted this form of bicycle. Although the basic design was still at an embryonic stage, and experiments continued to find improved materials and methods of manufacture, certain trends were noticeable. Weight was reduced by about 20 lbs., ladies' designs were becoming available and the plunger brake on the front tyre gave way to the manufacture of the roller lever rim brake. Another development

The Humber Lady-Front Tandem, c. 1898.

Inset: *Gazelle are one of the largest Dutch bicycle manufacturers. The first bicycle factory in Holland, Burgers Eerste Nederlandsche Rijewielen, was founded by Mr Burgers in 1870.*

Left: *An advertisement for bicycle lamps in Holland. As bicycling and cycling clubs became more popular at the turn of the century cyclists paid more attention to safety. There was an increase in the use of bicycle accessories such as bells and lamps.*

Soon after Dunlop's pneumatic tyre became available the Dutch developed their own brands. Vredestein took over the market in Holland and they still produce tyres today.

A Dutch advertisement for Dunlop's pneumatic tyre.

was the Bowden brake cable.

Until the middle of the 1890s oil lamps had been used almost exclusively on bicycles. The first successful versions were made specifically for Ordinaries from about 1876. These were called hub lamps as they fitted through the spokes of the large front wheel and clamped around the hub.

Among the more famous lamp manufacturers was Joseph Lucas, who, in 1872, established a small firm in Hockley near Birmingham.

To begin with the company sold household goods and lamp oil. With his sons, Harry and Christopher, Joseph then expanded into policemen's lamps, carriage lamps and money boxes. As the bicycle grew in popularity, the firm designed and patented, in 1879, an oil hub lamp purpose-made for the Ordinary. Over the years J. Lucas and Sons brought out a number of styles of hub lamp, and by the late 1880s cheaper versions were being made. By then Lucas had also patented an axle bearing for the hub lamp which made it easier for the lamp to remain still while the wheel was in motion. The bearing, in fact, consisted of a circular tube fastened tightly around the centre of the hub with a flange on each edge to prevent the lamp from moving sideways. Many other manufacturers jumped on the bandwagon, Salisbury, Miller, Albion, Powell and Hanmer being among the largest companies.

Lucas made several other types of cycle lamp similar to the hub lamp but with a parallel-sprung mounting bracket at the rear so that now machines other than Ordinaries could run at night. During the early years these lamps used petroleum oil mixed with whale oil, although there were in fact many types of oil on the market and all were virtually equally effective. With the advent of the Safety bicycle, Lucas developed what was to become the most famous of their oil-burning lamps, the "Silver King", which was patented in 1889 but not manufactured until 1896. The Silver King was as popular as the hub lamp, but it was neater, easier to clean and gave a very strong beam. Weighing 16½ oz. (dry), it burned with a ⅝-inch wick for about three hours. This was the first of a long line of lamps that set a model which contemporary firms were forced to follow.

A NOVEL IDEA. TO BRIGHTON AND BACK IN NO TIME.

THINGS ARE NOT ALWAYS WHAT THEY SEEM.

THE ABOVE IS NOT A COWARDLY ATTACK UPON AN UNPROTECTED LADY CYCLIST, BUT MERELY TOM GIVING HIS HEART'S IDOL HER FIRST LESSON.

Above left: *Cartoon from Punch 21 August 1869.* "A novel idea. To Brighton and back in no time."

Below left: *Cartoon from Punch, 15 August 1896.* "The above is not a cowardly attack upon an unprotected Lady Cyclist, but merely Tom giving his Heart's Idol her First Lesson."

Below: *John Player cigarette card – The Bicycle of the late '90s.*

The lamp was attached by a spring-loaded clamp which could be fitted to the head of the handlebars. This consisted of two parallel bars, sprung to give vertical shock-resistance to the body of the lamp when negotiating bumps. With the introduction of the pneumatic tyre, less vibration meant that there was no longer a need to retain a large wick and lamps became smaller.

By 1895 Lucas had switched almost completely to making bicycle lamps and accessories. Eventually the company began to produce cheaper lamps, made from steel rather than brass and copper. Between 1897 and 1904 they marketed a lamp especially for ladies. Called the "Microphote", it was oil-burning and weighed 9½ oz. This lamp was sold nickel-plated, as many Lucas lamps now were.

Oil remained the most commonly used fuel in cycle lamps until the turn of the century and "Britenwite" was the trade name given to the oil Lucas recommended its customers use in their lamps. Lucas also made their own lamp wicks in various sizes from ½ to 1⅛ inches. The firm then began to experiment with production of an acetylene lamp. An American company had already manufactured such a design, called the "20th Century" in 1888, although Lucas were not successful with acetylene lamps until 1901.

The 1890s also saw developments in transmission and by 1902, 86 per cent of the bicycles being made were fitted with freewheels. Gearing patents abounded around the turn of the century. Two of the more famous were the Sunbeam two-speed bracket gear with oil-bath gear case and the Sturmey-Archer three-speed hub gear. At this time gears were combined with a freewheel.

Experiments continued in other areas, too, with special consideration being paid to lightness, materials, components and accessories. Bamboo and wood were utilized, but although they were light they lacked strength. One successful and innovatory early lightweight bicycle was named after its creator – Mikael Pedersen.

Pedersen was a prolific inventor, who moved from Denmark to Dursley in Gloucestershire in 1893. When the initial backer of Pedersen's unique machine, Ernest Hooley, was declared bankrupt new management

John Player cigarette card of a lady cyclist wearing a Parisian divided skirt.

SUPPLEMENT TO VANITY FAIR

The Marchioness of Londonderry.
Mr W.H. Grenfell.
Mrs Sandford.

June. 11, 1896.

Vincent Brooks Day & Son Lith.

CYCLING IN HYDE PARK.

The Countess of Minto.

The Countess Cairns.

m Nevill.   Lady William Nevill.   Mrs W. H. Grenfell.

Lady Norreys.

Mrs Adrian Hope.   Lady Griffin.   Lady Alexander Kennedy.

Above: *Cycling in Hyde Park, from Supplement to Vanity Fair, 11 June 1896.*

71

came with the entry of the Lister family.

The Dursley Pedersen Cycle Co. was set up in the summer of 1899. The owners were Robert Ashton Lister, his son Charles, and Mikael Pedersen. However, in 1905 this company was wound up and the assets and liabilities taken over by R.A. Lister and Company Limited and the unique machine was produced once again but this time under the full control of the Lister family. The patent for Pedersen's design was accepted in 1894, with further improvements being approved in 1897 to the joints of the bicycle frame and the saddle, and an additional modification patented in 1900 which enabled the frame to be adapted for women.

The Dursley Pedersen bicycle was regarded as a de luxe machine, exhibiting superior efficiency and durability. It consisted of a completely triangular frame of light duplicated tubes, with a string and canvas hammock saddle slung between the front and back forks. The machine also had a two-speed hub gear, later upgraded to three-speed. After gaining considerable popularity, the model ceased manufacture around 1914 and Pedersen died in an old people's home in Denmark in 1929.

The "Naughty Nineties" as the 1890s came to be called, marked a social revolution in the use of the bicycle. By 1895 cycles were being patronized by every aristocratic and royal family in Europe and there were bicycle parties, gymkhanas and varied extravaganzas organized for the beau monde. Outside hotels in London uniformed boys waited to take bicycles from their titled owners. Society ladies paraded in the London parks. Her Ladyship would arrive in a brougham, with an attendant footman following in another carriage with her machine. Hostesses would open their annual balls with musical bicycle rides or enamel their bicycles to tone with the seasons.

Despite society patronage, however, there were still women who abhorred even the idea of their fellow sex labouring and sweating on a bicycle. Cycling for a woman was still regarded by many as immoral. Even so, it was no longer considered necessary for a chaperone to accompany a lady when she cycled, and with the 1890s craze there was an increase in manufacture not only of cheap machines but also of a variety of women's cycles. Although they had gained some freedom and mobility, women still had to fight to keep their independence, especially as regards the conventional and thoroughly ridiculous rules of the "proper attire".

Women could no longer separate cycling and fashion. Advocates of the divided skirt appeared early in the 1890s. This costume seems untroublesome now, yet critics then elbowed it for reasons that are unclear. What was needed, they argued, was a thoroughly well-cut cloth or serge skirt with the fullness falling equally on either side of the saddle. The hem should come just above the ankles and if the cyclist wished to walk as well she should do so in an ordinary skirt.

It was from abroad that the advances in women's cycling costume came. Rational dress, as it was known, was considered unconventional among many members of its own association who were fighting for radical changes in women's attire. In Paris, however, it was chic and modern, and resembled shooting dress, with a Norfolk-type jacket, a short skirt reaching only the knee and dark cloth leggings. Accessories included gauntlet gloves and a small cap. The more advanced women then adapted this costume by appearing in only the Norfolk jacket and the knickerbockers. They may have felt comfortable, but they caused consternation among onlookers.

Opposite: A picture of a wedding from the cover of Le Petit Journal, 28 March 1897.

The November edition of the 1890 *Cyclists' Touring Club Gazette* is full of arguments for and against this style of dress. One charming account by a lady cyclist of her recent trip to the Bois de Boulogne describes seeing a lady riding a Safety in dark green knickerbockers, white flannel shirt and band and tie with a near dark felt hat. "What is the ineradicable objection", she exclaimed, "to a woman appearing in sensible, comfortable two-legged garments? Are we not bipeds as well as men?" She went on to reflect, "I must confess I envied the plucky bicyclist, not only her comfortable costume, but her moral courage!" And she concluded her letter by stating that she wore knickerbockers whilst cycling, but was "still sufficiently under conventionality's tyranny" as she wore a long skirt over them!

American women were even less inhibited than their European counterparts. Already there was an established tradition of women's rights campaigning in the United States, where Amelia Bloomer and Elizabeth Cody Stanton were pressing for women's suffrage. In 1849 *Lily*, the first women's emancipation journal, was published.

It was not until 1892 that the first ladies' cycle club was founded in England – the Coventry Lady Cyclists. Also, in that same year the Lady Cyclists Association was instituted. Now women were openly organizing for the benefit of women alone.

The fashionable craze for cycling was short-lived among the upper classes. Serious cyclists scoffed at this sudden change of heart, which they had known would happen. But although the class barrier had not entirely disappeared cycling had become a social leveller. There was great camaraderie of the wheel evident in the 1890s. Cycling had become respectable, and apart from being pursued as a pastime in its own right, it could also be combined with other hobbies, such as painting, photography and sightseeing.

In 1896 there were at least five weekly journals for cyclists: *Cycling*, *The Cycle*, *The Cyclist*, *The Lady Cyclist* and *The Hub*. The great focal point of the cycling year was the Stanley Show. Each year the young men would gather to croon over the latest Safety, while the older men reminisced about the good old Ordinary.

John Player cigarette card showing a lady cyclist of 1896. By 1896 every third bicycle ordered was of the open-frame type for the lady rider.

There were still, however, a minority who treated cyclists with a degree of scorn and criticized the "scorcher" who insisted on tearing along in order to get there and back in the shortest time possible, or the lady who insisted on wearing the unconventional Rational costume whilst cycling.

One famous incident occurred at the Hautboy Hotel at Oakham in 1898 when Martha Sprague, the innkeeper, refused to serve Florence Harberton, the treasurer of the Rational Dress Association. The case came to court and the Cyclists' Touring Club supported Lady Harberton, who had been refused luncheon because she had been wearing Rational costume. Legal debate centred on whether Lady Harberton was guilty of indecent or improper conduct. It was reported that Mrs Sprague had said Lady Harberton could have luncheon in a private room but would have to pay for it. Lady Harberton had replied that she did not care, but just wished to be served as a Cyclists'

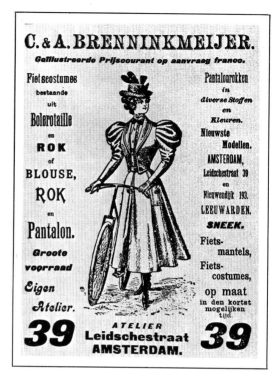

Touring Club member on the usual terms. Mrs Sprague had retorted that, in that case, she could go to the room on the other side of the bar, but that she would much rather Lady Harberton simply went away.

Lady Harberton was then taken in by way of the back door, where men were smoking and drinking in their working dress. She complained that the smell was abominable, that it was not a room for lunch and that she could not stay. Mrs Sprague said that was all she could offer, and as a result Lady Harberton rode to Cobham and had her lunch there.

When examined, Mrs Sprague said that she would never serve ladies in Rational costume unless they put on a skirt first. She had refused in the interests of her own business. In summing up, the chairman said that the question of whether ladies should or should not wear Rational dress was not in dispute. An innkeeper could not refuse to supply food because of the particular shape of a traveller's dress. The question at issue should be whether or not the guest could dictate which room to have lunch in. The innkeeper could select this provided it was a decent and proper room. The jury retired and returned a verdict of not guilty in favour of Mrs Sprague.

The number of Rationalists declined as the popularity of cyclists waned among weal-

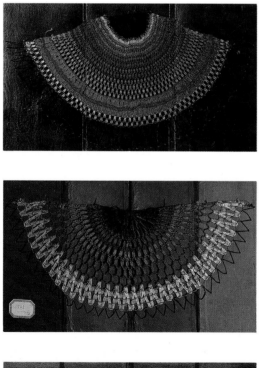

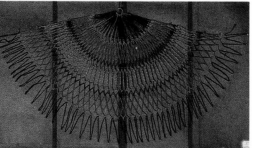

*S*kirt guards from the turn of the century.

The Safety Skirt Holder advertisement:

THE

Safety Skirt Holder

PATENT No 22437

PRICE ONE SHILLING

WITHOUT SKIRT HOLDER

WITH SKIRT HOLDER

*T*he majority of women coped with their long skirts by pinning them to the cycle, or sewing lead-shot into the hems. Charles Dawson took out this 1896 patent for elastic 'stirrups' to be sewn inside the skirt so that it was held down by the feet as the rider pedalled.

*B*icycle clubs were becoming increasingly popular in America. Harper's Weekly, 19 January, 1895.

Opposite: *A Raleigh Advertising Poster, 1922.*

Left: *An outing of the Cyclists Club of Paris.*

thier citizens. By 1905 hardly any ladies wore Rationals, but took to skirts considered to be short which were some four to eight inches off the ground in France and two to four in England.

Before the end of the century the cycle industry as a whole had expanded enormously. At the Stanley Show of 1895 there were 3,000 different models from 200 firms. Bicycles were now mass-produced on assembly lines with component manufacturers supplying standard fittings. Increased demand not only among the upper classes who were leaving their horses in the stables in order to take up cycling, but among the working people as well, meant that there was an expanding market for cheaper machines.

One success story of this period began with a Mr Frank Bowden and concluded with the Raleigh Cycle Company. At the age of 28, Bowden had arrived back in England from Hong Kong after being told that he had only a few months to live. He refused to accept the diagnosis, took up cycling and found, remarkably, that his health returned. Impressed by the cycle he had used, Bowden traced its manufacture to a small workshop in Raleigh Street, Nottingham. This small business was owned by Messrs Woodhead, Augois and Ellis and was turn-

ing out three bicycles per week. Bowden bought an interest in the company and injected his entrepreneurial spirit into it. Eventually, he became chairman.

The firm moved to a four-storey factory on Russell Street, Nottingham, and duly grew at a great rate. By 1896 Raleigh was occupying a purpose-built factory on a 7½-acre site in Faraday Road, Nottingham, and had achieved worldwide recognition for quality and design. However, Bowden continued to pursue possibilities and technical developments, especially the improvements in comfort brought about by Dunlop's pneumatic tyre. In 1902, Raleigh were approached by Henry Sturmey and James Archer, and as a result of their meeting a new department was created within the company to manufacture the new Sturmey-Archer gears.

Bowden was also quick to grasp the idea that the best way to promote Raleigh bicycles was to get champions across the finishing line riding them. He signed up many of the world's champions, providing them with both cycles and adequate backup. Raleigh thus became the first successful international commercial sponsors.

Around 1890 cycling as a sport was becoming widely accepted. It had first been

Below: *John Player cigarette card of the Simpson Lever-chain.*

Raleigh Cycle Company advertisement from a French catalogue, 1897.

Far right: Zimmerman aboard his 'Raleigh' racer.

included in the Olympic Games as early as 1886. Now pacing teams were set up and records beaten time and again.

In 1891 the many cycle races and speed trials at national level were brought under official control and speeds were authenticated. Main roads benefited from the attention of the new county councils. Good tracks were also coming into use, with fast surfaces at Crystal Palace, Paddington, Coventry, Long Eaton and, shortly afterwards, at Herne Hill.

The Safety bicycle was greatly boosted by racing, since it enabled men and women of any height to ride. Indeed, after 1891 there were no records passed for the Ordinary by the Roads Records Association, which had taken over adjudicating championships and track records from the National Cyclists' Union in 1888.

Women were also racing. The first timed ride by a woman is said to have been made by Tessie Reynolds, who made the journey from London to Brighton and back in 1893. Riding in Rational dress, Tessie completed the return trip in 8 hours and 38 minutes. In 1897 Maggie Foster completed the same run in 6 hours, 45 minutes and 9 seconds, only to lose the record a month later to a Mrs Ward. Mrs Ward in turn lost her record to Maggie Foster, who knocked the record down to 6 hours, 23 minutes and 58 seconds. Foster also rode on tracks at both Herne Hill and Crystal Palace. Paced by a motorcycle, she achieved over 30 miles in one hour.

One of American's leading cyclists was A.A. Zimmerman. In the 1880s he rode an American "Star" cycle, along with many U.S. riders, such as George Weber and Bert Owen, who attended the Harrogate Camp in 1883 and brought the first American Star over to England. The Star cycle employed the unique qualities of the high wheel bicycle, however, with this design the hind wheel had the greater diameter.

Patented in 1880 by G.W. Pressey of Hammonton, New Jersey, the original Star weighed 58 lb. and was not a success. A more practical design came from W.S. Kelley from Smithville, Burlington, New Jersey, in 1885. This machine was built by the H.B. Smith Machine Company of the same town. The driving mechanism of the Star involved two ratchet-and-rawl clutches, one each side of the wheel. A pawl on the wheel spindle engaged with one of the ratchet teeth inside the drum and the road wheel was rotated. On the upward stroke of the pedal the clutch went out of action.

A.A. Zimmerman rode for the New York Athletic Club. In 1892 he won the British National Championships at 1, 5 and 50 miles. During this same year Zimmerman rode a lightweight Raleigh specially built for use on the track. Made to measure, this machine weighed just 24 lb. The 1892 season saw Zimmerman start in 100 races, win 75 first prizes, take 10 seconds and 5 thirds, beating the record on seventeen occasions. In the first world championships, held in Chicago in 1893, he won the 1-mile and 10-kilometre titles. Zimmerman retained his amateur status until the close of 1893. He made his first appearance as a professional in July 1894.

The diamond frame was now established as the standard design both for the track and for the many enthusiastic cyclists who rode the length and breadth of the country. While nobody would claim that it had reached perfection, it does have ample strength, is light and pleasing to look at and not difficult to construct. Together with the pneumatic tyre, the diamond frame helped to bring about a huge expansion in cycling during this period, creating new possibilities for women and encouraging a fresh growth of interest in the bicycle.

Above: *A John Player cigarette card of the tandem of the '90s.*

LATER SAFETY BICYCLES: FROM 1900 TO WORLD WAR ONE

By the turn of the century the bicycle had assumed the form we know today. Commenting upon the fact that designers were now committed to the diamond frame, the editor of the 1901 *Cyclists' Touring Club Gazette* stated: "the cycle of to-day has reached a point so close to perfection that any real advance is most difficult." Having fixed on one basic shape, designers and manufacturers sought to perfect components, accessories and materials.

These manufacturers included the large established firms, such as B.S.A., Humber, Raleigh, Rudge-Whitworth, Triumph, New Hudson, Bayliss & Thomas, Alldays & Onions, and others. Standardized components were now supplied to these manufacturers by such companies as B.S.A., Eadie and Chater-Lea. William Chater-Lea had been a road racer of some renown. In 1890 he had begun to manufacture the component parts of racing bicycles. After a modest beginning with a handful of employees, the business developed a worldwide reputation for the design and manufacture of high-grade components. However, there still remained small, local manufacturers in many parts of the country.

A typical bicycle from this early twentieth-century period would have had a strong diamond frame, finished in hard stove enamel, with handlebars and wheelrims nickel-plated. The wheels would have been either 28 or 26 inches in diameter with bead-edged or pneumatic tyres.

The most popular brake of the time was a stirrup tyre which acted directly onto the rim of the wheel and was operated by roller handlebar levers or through Bowden cables. Some machines, had backpedalling brakes.

During this time there was a variety of hub gear units available. The epicyclic hub gear was the innovation of the 1890s, when William Reilly, a mechanic from Salford, Lancashire, applied for a patent in 1896, which was accepted in 1897. Reilly's hub gear was put into production by the Hub Two-Speed Gear Co. Limited of Collier Street, Greengate, Salford. The two-speed hub was a great success, and many improvements and patents were applied for during 1901 and 1906. Reilly soon fell out with the company and went to work for Royce of Manchester. It was while he was with Royce that he invented the three-speed gear. Of the many other men who had been toying with hub gears, the two most important at this time were James Archer and Henry Sturmey.

James Samuel Archer was born in 1854

Opposite: *Tandem at the seaside.*

A Gents Raleigh, c. 1900.

Above: *Lady's Humber, c. 1900.*

Below: *Raleigh Cross-frame Tandem, c. 1905.*

with the Hub manufacturing company.

Contention apart, however, the three-speed hub appeared in 1902 with a consolidated claim from the ranks of Sturmey, Archer, Reilly, Mills and Pellant. George Pilkington Mills was a record-breaking cyclist and Raleigh works manager who was eventually given the task of mass-producing the new gear.

In 1903 the 3-Speed Syndicate was established to produce the new hub, following an agreement between Pellant, Bowden, Reilly and Archer. A second agreement between Raleigh and the Syndicate stated that the new gear was to be manufactured by Raleigh but not exclusively for use on Raleigh cycles. A decision was then made to call the gear the "Sturmey-Archer", a simple combination of the names of the two patentees. The year 1903 saw the launch of the first Sturmey-Archer three-speed gear. It was an instant success and gained a growing reputation.

In 1903, the 3 October edition of *Cycling* contained a long article on variable speed gears, which described the Sturmey-Archer three-speed as the invention of Sturmey and Archer. Mills and Pellant received no credit and Reilly was only mentioned in so far as improvements were concerned.

A great speed-gear competition then ensued, with specialist hub gears being produced by manufacturers, such as B.S.A., John Marston Sunbeams and Lea Francis. Lea Francis was the company formed by R.H. Lea and G.I. Francis. Both men had been with the Singer Company and went into partnership to manufacture bicycles at Lower Ford Street, Coventry. They first exhibited at the 1895 Stanley Show. In 1905 their manager F.A. Griffin designed a two-speed hub gear, followed by a three-speed model in 1908. Both were fitted with Lea Francis freewheels. Lea Francis remained committed to good design and high-quality workmanship until they ceased bicycle production in 1914.

Albert Eadie also patented a two-speed hub gear in 1903, and Villiers produced their two-speed one year earlier. The year 1904 saw the introduction of the elaborate two-speed, Sunbeam bracket gear, encased within an oil-bath chaincase; and by 1907 a total of almost thirty systems had been introduced.

and died in 1920. He was a fellow workman at Royce with Reilly. Henry Sturmey was born in 1857, in Somerset. He was famous for his publication *The Indispensable Bicyclists' Handbook*, which had sold out within a month of publication. His second book was called *Sturmey's Indispensable Handbook to the Safety Bicycle*. Sturmey was also the editor of *The Cyclist* magazine and chief consultant to the Bicyclists' Touring Club. Doubts have been voiced as to whether or not Reilly was behind Archer, who only filed the patents for him because of his contract

車行自跑海上刻新

永和德畫店

An alternative gear had now evolved which depended on the driving chain moving between different-diameter sprockets. This owed something to the "Gradient" chain gear of 1899, and originated in France in about 1909. In the 1920s it was named the "Derailleur".

By 1908 the all-speed gear was still undergoing development. It was lightened, strengthened and generally improved upon. New patents were applied for by rivals in Germany and America. Although they guarded their British patent rights, Sturmey-Archer were also keen to capitalize on their overseas patents. In 1905 Bowden had negotiated with Messrs Dubied of France and the Aachen Company of Germany. It was not until 1912 that terms were offered to Morris Russell & Co., USA, and in 1914 an agreement was made with Sears Roebuck & Company of Chicago for use of Sturmey-Archer's American patents. In 1914 some 20,000 Raleigh bicycles were factory-fitted with Sturmey-Archer gears (about one-third of Bowden's total production). With the advent of World War I Sturmey-Archer was requisitioned for the war effort and by the close of the war very few manufacturers were in business. Speed gears were now mainly Sturmey-Archer or B.S.A..

The period between 1900 and the Great War saw the introduction of many accessories and improvements in bicycle design. New accessories included bells, mudguards, carriers, pumps, repair outfits and lamps.

By 1901 experiments with acetylene were becoming more successful; Lucas manufactured such a lamp called the "Luminator". However, in 1902 Joseph Lucas died of typhoid and the business passed on to his son Harry. In 1903 came the acetylene lamp design which was to prove the first in a long line. The "Acetyphote" had a carbide bowl situated beneath the water container and a separate housing for the burner and reflector. This lamp was produced until 1914.

At the beginning of World War I rear

The first cyclists in Shanghai, 1900.

85

Opposite: *Mars-Räder Advertising Poster of 1904.*

Inset: *Badenia Advertising Poster of 1910.*

Below: *Lady's Rover, c. 1906.*

lights for cyclists became compulsory. Both oil and acetylene were used, with the acetylene head lamp generating enough gas to service the rear via a rubber tube.

In 1904 practical electrical lighting in the form of a dynamo had been introduced, but it was not until 1912 that Lucas made a set. By 1914 lamp manufacturers such as Lucas had entered the field of car accessories and electric lighting production. With the outbreak of war, however, the resources of Lucas, like those of many companies, were devoted to the production of munitions.

Although the diamond frame was victorious in the final battle for design supremacy, many well-known firms exhibited cross-framed machines during this period, and among such novelties the featherweights reigned supreme. The Pedersen model had been the first to demonstrate the full potential of the extremely light bicycle. Raleigh, during this period, produced a cross-frame featherweight with weighed 26½ lb. and other such designs were manufactured by Centaur and Humber. Popular cross-frame tandems included the Raleigh and Referee.

Not only cross frames, but also spring frames were still well represented at the shows, and continued to be made by such companies as B.S.A., Enfield and James. The James Cycle Company was founded by Harry James. In 1881 he had begun the manufacture of the Ordinary in a small factory on Birmingham's Constitution Hill. James, like many others, was quick to

appreciate the advantages of the Safety bicycle and the pneumatic tyre. After moving to new, larger premises at Sparkbrook, he began to produce an excellent Safety. An early James model had a long head tube, and a sloping top tube, incorporating the seat cluster method of brazed-up seat stays in place of a bolt-pinning attachment. The James was a popular mount for society cyclists. In 1897 the company was floated, and shortly afterwards Harry James resigned from his position as managing director due to illness. However, he retained a link as consulting engineer to the company. The then manager, Hyde, promoted the incorporation of the freewheel into the machines, by producing a reasonably priced and reliable component, patented in 1900. In 1908 a new James plant was opened at Greet, on the outskirts of Birmingham; and at the Franco-British exhibition, the firm was awarded the gold medal for excellence of production. During World War I James produced thousands of bicycles and motorcycles for the forces, before returning to the manufacture of bicycles, tricycles and tandems in peacetime.

The best place to view the new machines was, as always, the yearly show. At the 1901 Stanley Show, Rudge-Whitworth occupied a central place in the hall. The *Cyclists' Touring Club Gazette*, commenting upon the show realised that the company had drawn a line between racers and tourers, and had "Placed upon the market a racing machine which is not intended for use upon the road". In 1903 Rudge-Whitworth became "By Royal Warrant Cycle Manufacturers to His Majesty King Edward VII".

The Rudge-Whitworth company had begun in 1869–70 when Dan Rudge of Wolverhampton built his own bicycles. This he continued to do for the following ten to eleven years. On 26 June 1880, Dan Rudge died at Wolverhampton and Mr Woodcock, a Coventry solicitor, who knew of Rudge's reputation, bought the goodwill from his widow and took the name to Coventry as "D. Rudge & Co.", later to be known as the "Rudge Cycle Co. Ltd". A Mr C. Vernon Pugh was duly asked if his father would allow parts of his factory, the Whitworth works, that were currently unused to be given over to cycle manufacture. This was

agreed in 1891, and C.V. Pugh became general manager. After Mr Woodcock's death, the two firms amalgamated into the Rudge-Whitworth Company.

The Stanley Show had been established in 1878 when the Stanley Bicycle Club members had exhibited their own new machines of that year. In 1890 the cycle manufacturers' Trade Protection Association was founded, and in 1893 they promoted a National Show at Crystal Palace. The Stanley Show was established at the Agricultural Hall. The National Show lasted only ten years and the Stanley Show was superseded by the Union Show at Olympia in 1910.

The year 1902 saw the fourth Exposition Internationale de l'Automobilia de Cycle and des Sports – the Paris Show. A typical French bicycle of this period was a poor copy of the typical American model. Some were built up of B.S.A. parts. Other manufacturers who exhibited at the Paris shows included Griffon, Vauzelle, Marelle & Co., Plaison, Peugeot Frères and Pliante, whose bicycles, used in the French army, had two parallel backbones connecting the head with a curved seat tube, the backbones being jointed for folding purposes. Cycling lost some of its prominence in America during this period. In 1875 over 250 manufacturers were in existence, but by 1917 only a small number remained, among them such companies as Columbia, Crescent, Cleveland and Waverly. Several foreign manufacturers were seen in the United States, including

*C*hilds Tricycle from 1916.

B.S.A., Rudge and the French Peugeot, but it was not really until Greg Lemond's 1986 win in the Tour de France that cycling sprang again into prominence in America.

During the years between the turn of the century and World War I there were experiments with frame materials, such as aluminium alloys and titanium. In the February 1911 edition of the *Cyclists' Touring Club Gazette* there was considerable discussion about aluminium alloys. F.T. Bidlake, in his "Current Comments" commended the reduction in weight of bicycles, when standard roadsters were "So tending to grossness", but he also stated rather tentatively that "it is not by any means certain that the new aluminium alloy would be serviceable".

Quality bicycles during this period were represented by the de luxe machines, of which the Marston Golden Sunbeam was classed as the "Rolls Royce" of the cycling world. A 1910 advertisement in *Cycling* for John Marston's Sunbeam bicycles depicted a thoroughbred horse with the caption: "A thoroughbred Cycle" and "Built where no low grade cycles are bred". Made by John Marston & Company of Wolverhampton, the Sunbeam was manufactured from the best materials and included such features as an oil-bath chaincase and two-speed epicyclic gear. The Sunbeam first appeared in 1887, to be followed in 1900 by the Golden Sunbeam, which remained in production until the demise of the company in 1936.

There were also experiments with recumbent bicycles and small-wheeled bicycles during this period. The first patent for a recumbent bicycle was applied for in 1896 by an American called I.F. Wales. However, designs of this kind did not represent any real advance. The probable forerunner of the modern-day low-profile racing machine was seen as early as 1902, when such models were designed with a shorter steering-head with a sloping top tube, from the seat lug to the top of the head. Many were fitted with Eadie, B.S.A. or Chater-Lea components.

The 1910 racing machines intended for serious road use could have been fitted with wooden rims and tubular tyres. Variable gears were hardly used at all, and the three-speed hub was exploited only on hilly courses. However, in the main pre-1914 speedmen were content with the fixed gear.

Far left: *Styria Advertising Poster, 1905.*

Left: *Opel Advertising Poster, 1908.*

Below left: *Wanderer Advertising Poster, 1905.*

Below: *Mars das Qualitäts-Rad Advertising Poster, 1925.*

Derailleurs had not, as yet, invaded the domain of road racing.

Many great races were run and records broken during the period. Among the best-known of the longer events up to twelve hours were the Anchor Shield and the Cawardine Cup. In 1908 W.J. Pett broke the one-hour record with 30 miles 1,170 yards, a record he held for 21 years.

Records were not broken solely by men. Mary Catherine Green (Kate Green) from Yorkshire was not only one of the first ladies in the North to wear Rationals, she was also a great competitor, whose heyday ran from 1905 to 1908. In August 1908 she rode a 24-hour trial, unpaced, and covered 308 miles. In September 1909 she covered 313 miles, over the same time.

However, the greatest test of strength and stamina originated in 1903 and is still, to-day, a source of pleasure for millions of people either viewing at home on their television sets or by the side of the roads in France. The Tour de France was the dream of one man, Henri Desgrange, who in 1903 organized a cycle race around France. For the first Tour there were 78 entries and 60 starters. The race was six stages long and only 21 riders finished the full 2,428 kilometres. The winner was Maurice Garin, who was 2 hours, 49 minutes and 3 seconds ahead of his nearest rival. Garin won the first stage from Paris to Lyon. Aucauturier won the next two, from Lyon to Marseille and from Marseille to Toulouse. Laeser took Toulouse to Bordeaux but Garin won the last two stages, Bordeaux to Nantes and then Nantes to Ville d'Avray.

The race caught the public's imagination – they marvelled at the strength and stamina of the competitors and the great distance involved. The following year the Tour was raced over the shortest distance in its history at 2,388 kilometres. Henri Carnet, the winner, was only 20 years of age. That same year the Tour provoked heightened emotions, with rival supporters clashing at St Etienne and road blocks on the final stage to Paris. Even so, a third Tour was staged, with Louis Trousselier the winner, although the demonstrations continued.

In 1905 Desgrange took the Tour through mountains for the first time, with the 3,900-foot climb of Ballon d'Alsace. In 1906 only

14 finished out of 82, and in 1909 the first non-Frenchman won, Luxembourg's Francois Faber. His victory coincided with a break in the winning run of the Peugeot team, and for the next four years the team prize went to Alcyant. Peugeot had been established by Henri and Ernest Peugeot, who in 1887 were manufacturing spring-steel hoops for women's crinoline dresses. Armand Peugeot had visited Britain in 1882 and seen the large numbers of cyclists; and when he returned to France he decided to manufacture cycles of his own.

In 1910 the Tour journeyed through the Pyrenees for the first time, and in 1911 Desgrange took the race to the Galiber, a climb of some 8,000 feet. The following year saw the first Belgian to win the Tour, Odile

Above: The Start of the Grand Prix in Paris in 1906.

Opposite: Nederlandsche Kroon Rijwielen advertising poster.

Below: Lady's Golden Sunbeam.

Opposite: *Around the map are shown the winners from 1903 to 1936. (The race was not run during 1915–19).*

Defraye. However, between 1915 and 1918 the Tour was not run because of the outbreak of World War I.

The history of military cycling may be said to have commenced in 1887 when a Colonel Stracey realized that bicycle-riders could be useful for reconnaissance and similar military work, including despatching information. The Colonel obtained co-operation from other enthusiasts, including a Colonel Savile. Communications were sent to various volunteer corps requesting all volunteers who were cyclists to attend manoeuvres that Easter, to see if the scheme was viable. Ordinaries, early Safeties and tricycles were all ridden, and the observers were very impressed. The matter was put before the War Office and on 1 April 1888 the first military volunteer cycling corps, the 26th Middlesex, was founded, although unfortunately no financial assistance towards its support was forthcoming from the government. Eventually, any volunteer corps was at liberty, if it could, to raise a cycling section, which had to be at least twenty-one strong – twenty men and one officer. Be-

cause there was no government subsidy, the volunteers could choose their own machines, although they had to be of a standard design, strong and durable, between 25 and 30 lb. in weight, and fitted with a brake and mudguards. The machine would then be stamped for duty. However, before entering a cycling corps the cyclist would have first undergone the regulation infantry drill after which he would participate in special cycling training.

The Boer War (1899–1902) gave the cyclists an opportunity to prove themselves, not only in the home defence mode envisaged for them by the War Office but also in the field of South Africa, where their main duties were despatch-riding or the reconnoitre of roads for transporters.

The premier model used for this purpose was the B.S.A. folding Safety bicycle. This same design was also employed in large numbers in World War I (1914–1918), although the majority of cyclist units during this war were to be turned into infantry.

On 7 November 1914, a Royal Warrant authorized the formation of a corps of cyc-

Below: *Spectators cheering on competitors in the Tour de France.*

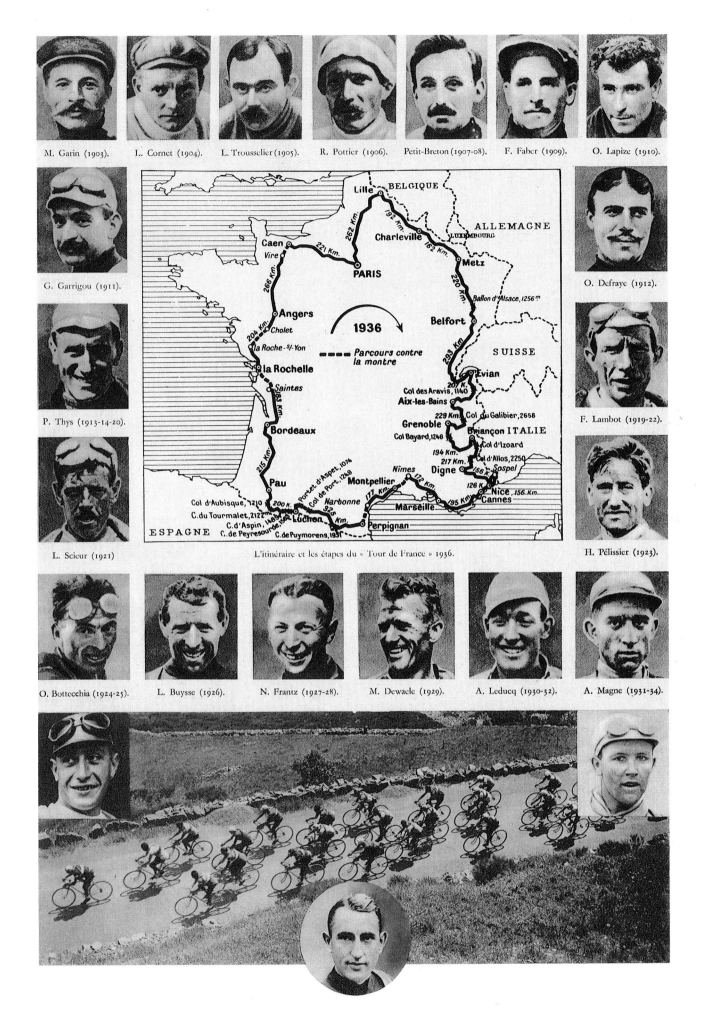

M. Garin (1903).   L. Cornet (1904).   L. Trousselier (1905).   R. Pottier (1906).   Petit-Breton (1907-08).   F. Faber (1909).   O. Lapize (1910).

G. Garrigou (1911).

O. Defraye (1912).

P. Thys (1913-14-20).

F. Lambot (1919-22).

L. Scieur (1921)

H. Pélissier (1923).

L'itinéraire et les étapes du « Tour de France » 1936.

O. Bottecchia (1924-25).   L. Buysse (1926).   N. Frantz (1927-28).   M. Dewaele (1929).   A. Leducq (1930-32).   A. Magne (1931-34).

93

lists to be entitled the "Army Cyclist Corps". Each army corps was supplied with a battalion of such cyclists, who were used in the field campaigns of France and Belgium.

In the December 1916 edition of the *Cyclists' Touring Club Gazette*, a Lance-Corporal A.S. gives an account of practice manoeuvres in this country for a cyclist battalion, which he describes as being a "mobile and useful branch of the army". These "Khaki-clad Cyclists" with their strong, heavy machines had to carry arms and ammunition strapped to themselves and their mounts. With a "Prepare to mount!" the cyclists would be awheel and advancing until a bugle sounded the signal to "Detach Arms" followed by the command "Stack Cycles!" The cyclists would then fall out until the bugle sounded again for them to "Fall In" and "Unstack Cycles!" By the close of World War I, however, many of these Army Cyclists Corps had been demobilized or disbanded.

Above: *A platoon of Belgian soldiers equipped with cycles, August 1914.*

Left: *A folding bicycle made by Gerard in 1893.*

Opposite: *Photograph showing the climb up Mount Galibier in the Tour de France.*

The Modern Bicycle

LEIGH

-STEEL BICYCLE

LATER SAFETY BICYCLES:
THE INTERWAR YEARS

The First World War had created a decline in cycling. This decline was further hastened by the advent of the motor car, which gradually put paid to the use of the bicycle as reductions in price made cars more accessible to more people. Attention now switched to discrediting these new demons who were spoiling the roads. However, cycling was about to enter a new phase. By the late 1920s it had become an affordable pastime for the majority, and the 1930s marked a golden age of touring, with towns and villages warmly welcoming the cyclists, who contributed to the rural economy as they rode from one watering hole to another.

Although the basic design of the bicycle remained comfortably unaltered for many years, progress did continue after the war in relation to materials, construction and quality. The basic requirements had not changed for many years, and lightness, neatness and greater efficiency were still eagerly sought after. Chromium-plating, for example, was used instead of nickel-plating (which proved more durable), comfortable saddles became available and 26-inch diameter tyres were used.

An editorial for the 1924 Olympia Show commented on the lack of innovation in these post-war years: "Detail improvements will be observed in many directions, but design has necessarily become stereotyped to a considerable extent." However, the most satisfactory development was the "increasing attention given to light machines and many fine specimens will be on view".

Rudge-Whitworth were just one firm which exhibited a lightweight machine in the mid-1920s. This was equipped with a three-speed hub gear and weighed 33 lb. Light-

Opposite: Raleigh Advertising Poster, 1922.

Left: Rush hour brings a big crowd to the main street in Peking. Bicycles are still the most popular means of individual transport in Chinese cities. Chinese makes of bicycle have such poetic names as White Dove, Everlasting and Phoenix.

Below: A bicycle parking area near Peking's Department Store.

Opposite: *The Dürkopp Diana Advertising Poster, 1915.*

Right: *In Holland in the 1930s there was one bicycle for every two members of the population.*

weight designs were being introduced for both touring and racing. They incorporated a shorter wheelbase and a more upright steering-head with 26-inch diameter wheels and tyres. Celluloid was used for such items as mudguards, chaincases and chainguards.

There was a thriving correspondence in the press on the subject of lightweight cycles, with the riders of the heavier touring cycle being dubbed the "dreadnoughts". In the

Below: *A Gent's Golden Sunbeam.*

November 1924 edition of the *Cyclists' Touring Club Gazette* a V. Bail G. Malan wrote in favour of the lightweights as opposed to the dreadnoughts: " . . . scrap your dreadnoughts and go in for a light-roadster; you will then realise to the full the joy of cycling!"

However, it was not until 1932 that the lightweight cycle had its own show. The Lightweight Cycle Show was organized by Mr J.E. Holdsworth (on behalf of Cycling Exhibitions Limited) and was held at the Royal Horticultural Hall, Vincent Square, Westminster. Unfortunately, it only lasted until 1935. The Olympia Cycle Show made its farewell appearance in 1936 and reflected on the progress achieved following the famine caused by the war. By the mid-1930s cheaper, lighter and livelier mounts were available. The manufacturers of bicycles began to be concentrated with the larger, established firms, such as Raleigh, where cycles were mass-produced. At the beginning of World War I Raleigh had been turning out 50,000 cycles a year. Half of their capacity was then turned over to munitions and they made a major contribution to the war effort. In 1921 Sir Frank Bowden died

and was replaced by one of his sons, Harold, under whose management the company continued to grow in spite of the change in direction necessitated by the war effort.

The year 1925 saw the introduction of the Raleigh lower bottom bracket, which enabled the rider to put his feet on the ground. Raleigh absorbed Humber in 1932, and in 1936 the Raleigh frictionless "Dynohub" was designed, which generated its own electricity. In the years leading up to World War II Raleigh became renowned for the production of motorcycles, a three-wheeled light car and delivery vans. At the outbreak of World War II production suffered severely until the company was able to put its postwar recovery plan into action.

The 1920s and 1930s proved to be a period of subtle improvements, and the needs of the cyclist were carefully considered. The cycling magazines carried a great deal of correspondence regarding such ideas as derailleur gears, aluminium alloys, lightweight cycles and dynamo lighting.

The general design of speed gears remained unchanged, but considerable improvements were seen in respect of the working principles. Following World War I there was a shortage of raw materials. However, it did not take Sturmey-Archer long to resume production of their X-type gear, and shortly afterwards the company

were marketing a new speed gear – the "K" three-speed gear. In 1921 Henry Sturmey applied for a patent for the first five-speed hub gear. Raleigh rejected the design and the Sturmey company had difficulty manufacturing the product. Unfortunately, Sturmey himself died in 1930 without actually seeing it produced.

The 1920s were busy years for Sturmey-Archer, as they continued to increase their overseas interests. In 1924 their trade mark was registered in Australia, the following year in Japan. In terms of innovation, however, the decade proved less fruitful, and in fact no new patents were taken out for Sturmey-Archer gears.

Although the three-speed hub was still popular with tourers, racing cyclists were growing discontented with their lot. Another subject which provoked discussion in the cycling press was the suitability of hub gears for tandems.

In France, in 1928, Lucian Juy patented a unit of some importance. Juy was the founder of "Simplex" and the inventor of the double pivot derailleur system. During the 1930s competition from the derailleur units now being made dictated that Sturmey-Archer resume experiments into a lighter hub with closer ratios.

In 1930 Tuillo Campagnolo had patented a derailleur system and in 1931 W. Hill had patented the "Tri-Velox" (an early type of derailleur), a three-speed gear in which ratios were changed via three sprockets of different diameter on the rear wheel hub. These early campaigners for derailleur units were soon followed by other manufacturers, such as Villiers. By the mid-1930s a number of improved derailleurs were manufactured, such as the "Cyclo" systems. It was in answer to these developments and the growing popularity of derailleur systems, that in the mid-1930s Sturmey-Archer produced a single epicyclic three-speed hub with wide, medium and close ratios. During 1938 they also created a double epicyclic hub gear with wide, medium and close ratio designs.

Trigger controls for gears were improved as well. These were mounted on the handlebars and proved more convenient than the old-style mounting on the top tube. This new design became the basis for all such controls until the mid-1980s. By the close of the 1930s

Sturmey-Archer had introduced a different type, which consisted of a quick-release gear control cable connection. This connection could be broken by displacing one section out of line.

The 1930s also saw an increased interest in dynamo lighting and the dynohub dynamo concept. During World War I rear lights had been compulsory. In the post-war years they were retained "on the advice of experts" and much to the chagrin of many cyclists, correspondence flew between pro-rear-light cyclists and those against them. Although a good range of oil and acetylene lamps remained available during the inter-war years, they were gradually being replaced by electric systems. The simplest electric lamps were battery-operated, but these were not so convenient as those fuelled by a dynamo, which generated sufficient current for both head and tail lamps. The dynohub was also popular for a while. This consisted of a compact electric lighting generator incorporated within the wheel hub. In 1937 Sturmey-Archer had produced a six-volt dynohub.

The majority of bicycles during the period were fitted either with calliper or with coaster brake systems. With the calliper system a Bowden wire controlled a rim brake. This cantilever brake exerted pressure directly onto each hub. The coaster design was an internally expanding system incorporated within a hub, such as the Sturmey-Archer or Chater-Lea. This type of brake was more expensive.

As these more sophisticated improvements were introduced, a new era was ushered in – the age of the cycling family had arrived, with a flourish of sidecars, trailers, kiddie-seats and tandems.

The tandem achieved new peaks of popularity over the years between the late 1920s and the 1950s. The models of this time were now lighter and more efficient than previous designs, although components and frame tubing remained stronger and heavier than those on solo machines. Special light tandems were produced for racing and record attempts, while the more favoured model for touring proved to the double gents' model, which could also be readily used by ladies wearing trousers or shorts, in either the front or the rear riding position.

An advocate of the sidecar was a lady with the pen-name "Petronella". Petronella first appeared in the *Cyclists' Touring Club Gazette* in 1929 with several popular short stories about her life on the wheel, camping, motherhood and touring for women. Her common-sense attitudes and wise comments were soon accorded a permanent place within the *Gazette* and "Wheelwisdom for Women" first appeared in October 1930. She was extremely popular, although elder members scorned her for her modern ways. Petronella (alias Mrs E. Parkes) begun her official work in the club in 1921 as Honorary Press Secretary to the Birmingham D.A., a

Above: *F.H.R. Grubb Touring Cycle, c. 1929.*

Below: *Triumph Moller, c. 1943.*

A lworth triplet with Watsonian sidecar, 1930s.

J ohn Player cigarette card of a lady cyclist, 1939.

position in which she proved equally successful, and through her work she began to popularize the juvenile sidecar movement. In 1932 she won the Sir Alfred Bird Memorial Prize, awarded for "the most singular service" rendered to the club.

Since World War I there had been a gradual influx of women into club life. As conventional barriers were broken in relation to women's dress, bloomers grew shorter and shorter until the 1930s when shorts were accepted without much complaint. Many clubs boasted a battalion of cycling women, their short bobbed hair covered by a beret, wearing a variety of costume ranging from divided skirts to short skirts, breeches, bloomers and shorts (only a few inches above the knee), with herringbone-patterned knee socks.

Even so, correspondence concerning the correct attire for women still raged in the cycling press – not that it would have swayed many minds on the subject. Indeed, many letters were simply about how to look dignified with an underskirt showing under a rising shorter skirt. In the April 1928 edition of the *Cyclists' Touring Club Gazette* a

"Miss 1927" wrote regarding troublesome underskirts: "Whilst on a tour down West on becoming warm I have discarded my skirt and ridden through the country in a petticoat, . . . I felt quite cool and refreshed, and did not care a jot what anyone thought."

Men did not have to deal with such problems. Their cycling garb had always been sensible, and they now rode in shorts, knickers (which were not so full as plus-fours) or plus-fours. However, they still became entangled in the arguments. In the August 1928 edition of the *Gazette*, James O. Haydin had the answer to the problem of petticoats: "If petticoats are such troublesome things, I should advise cycling ladies to leave them off and be satisfied with a skirt." The real answer, of course, was to become a "shortist", take off the skirt altogether and don a sensible, cool pair of shorts!

As the numbers of women in cycling associations increased, more of them became involved in long- and short-distance touring, in tandem-riding, sprints and road racing. The cycles these women rode were less cumbersome, because they did not have to be constructed with heavy voluminous clo-

The winners of a ladies' event at a bicycle rally in Paris, 1897.

A Womens Cycling Club in England.

thing in mind. In fact, some machines weighed as little as 27 lb.

As women proved themselves again and again on both track and field, prejudice was soon dispelled. In 1925 Mrs Du Heaume was the only woman in a field of 24 to ride in the Reading Wheelers "12". She came third with a total distance of 197¾ miles. In 1927 the Rosslyn Ladies Cycling Club was formed and Mrs Du Heaume won the twelve-hour event promoted by the club with a distance of just over 205 miles.

Several women accomplished great feats but no permanent official record of their times and distances was kept. Many considered this to be unfair; and with the rapidly increasing interest shown by women in the sporting side, action was definitely needed. Time and time again efforts were made to persuade the Roads Records Association officials to allow women to ride for records, but to no avail.

Eventually in October 1934, a small body of enthusiasts, including Petronella, met to form the Women's Road Records Association. In essence this was a group of private members and affiliated clubs set up to verify and certify the best performances recorded by women riders. Petronella was nominated President and Mrs Du Heaume, among others, was made an official. The association

*M*arguerite Wilson won over fifty medals and trophies. This photograph shows a training run. She is carrying a bottle of milk on her machine.

'*Marguerite Wilson, the Hercules cycling wonder girl professional, setting off during the night, after a snack, during her Land's End to John O'Groats record-breaking attempt'.* Hercules Cycle & Motor Company.

formulated rules, recognized twelve place-to-place and distance records, decided on standard times, published a handbook and designed a badge. By February 1935, there were 50 members.

Many record attempts resulted and first holder of a Women's Road Records Association record was Lilian Dredge, who, riding a Claude Butler, achieved a total of six records, including the "End-to-End" and the "1,000".

The year 1938 saw the appearance of an outstanding lady rider of great ability. Her name was Marguerite Wilson. Marguerite raised the Women's Road Records Association records to such an extremely high level, that amateur and professional classes had to be separated. However, the association continued to work efficiently for all women riders who wished to make an attempt on a record, regardless of their class.

A significant development for racing bicycles during this period was the butted tube. The theory behind this process was that the tubing of the frame takes less strain in the middle than at the ends. It was therefore possible to make a racing cycle lighter, and thus increase its efficiency, by making it thinner in the middle. A racing machine constructed with butted steel tubing could weigh as little as 15 lb.

For over ninety years, the Reynolds Company have been at the forefront of cycle-frame production. Their successful history began in the suburbs of Birmingham, where in 1898 Alfred Milward Reynolds patented

Below: *Baines Whirlwind, c. 1936.*

the "butting" process and founded the Patent Butted Tube Company. In 1930 the "531" tube was introduced and in 1938 Reynolds were given the Cyclists' Touring Club award for this brand as "the most significant contribution to cycling". A cycle frame built in Reynolds 531 was ridden to victory in the 1958 Tour de France, the first of 27 such victories up to 1988. The 531 has,

in fact, been ridden by the most famous names in racing, including Antequetil, Merckx, Hinault, Thevenet, Fignon, Lemond and Doyle.

In 1976 Reynolds introduced "753", a new concept in cycle-frame tubes and 50 per cent stronger than any of its competitors; and in 1982 the company added yet another new type of material to its range in the form of the "501". Until this point all Reynolds materials had been produced from manganese molybdenum steels, due to their ability to maintain their strength after applying heat. In 1987 came the launch of "653", the first set to offer tubes of variable strengths specifically designed for professional races, and a new concept in obtaining strength and stiffness where it is needed most in the frame geometry. Butted tubes were eventually manufactured by other firms including the "Kromo" variety by Accles and Pollock Limited, made in chrome molybdenum.

The late 1920s and 1930s saw a host of top-class riders in Britain, including Theaker, White, Sibbit, Green, Cozens and Chambers, to name only a few. During the 1930s an Australian captured many hearts with his brilliant riding. In 1934 Hubert

B.S.A. folding paratroop cycle, c. 1936.

The start of a cycle race by the River Seine.

Top left: *M. Southall, F. Southall and C. Hallermeak after breaking the one mile triplet record in 1930.*

Top right: *Harry and Percy Wylds, winners of the Madison Race.*

Left: *F.W. Southall about to start a race. He is wearing a spare tyre around his shoulders.*

Opperman broke five records in two epic rides. His plan was to make a general onslaught on English records, including his 1,000 miles (an extension of the end-to-end), riding a B.S.A. cycle with Cyclo derailleur gears. However, the greatest rivalry, which produced classic races during this period, was promoted between Harry Wyld and Frank Southall.

Between the wars a family of four racing brothers from Derby made an important contribution to British racing history. As a team from 1926 to 1928, Frederick Henry (Harry), L. Arthur, Percy and Ron Wyld won the National Pursuit Championship for the Derby R.C.C. Individually, they were all superb riders, although Harry stood above the others and was soon to become the idol of the crowd, racing on a golden taper tube Selbach. In 1924 he won his first national championship title, while he alone also held every other individual title – the 50-mile in 1927, the ¼-mile, 5-mile and 25-mile in 1928. As a sprint champion and stayer he broke many tandem-paced and motor-paced records and represented his country internationally on road and track, achieving a bronze medal in the 1924 Olympic Games 50-kilometre race held in Paris and another bronze in the 1928 Games in Amsterdam as a member of the British pursuit team.

Frank Southall also rode in the 1928 Olympia Games, along with Percy and L. Arthur Wyld, Sibbit, Chambers, Cozens, Turner and Kerridge. Southall was the greatest British all-round cyclist of his generation. Riding for the Norwood Paragon Cycle Club, he began his successful career in 1921 and held the world unpaced standing-start track records at 1, 5, 10 and 25 miles. For the one-hour (unpaced) record he covered 26 miles 838 yards. Southall won every classic road open event as well, including hill climbs, and broke records at 25, 50 and 100 miles. He represented his country in the 1925 and 1926 championships and at two Olympiads, the 1928 in Holland and the 1932 in Los Angeles, when he was involved in spectacular clashes with his greatest Olympic rival, the Dane Henry Hansen. Southall also rode tandem successfully with his brother Monty and with A.R. Watkins, Frank Cleeve and Stan Butler.

Major developments in cycle-racing at this time began in 1922, when the Road Racing Council took over the running of time trials. The world championships began in England but, due to bad weather and poor organization they were completed in Paris. The year 1934 saw the introduction of cycling to the Empire Games (now known as the Commonwealth Games), and in 1937 the Road Racing Council was renamed the Road Time Trials Council, the current governing body for British time trials.

In France, after World War I had ended, Desgrange was keen to get the Tour de France started again. He suggested that the race leader should have a yellow jersey to identify him from the rest and the *maillot jaune* still indicates the leader today. In 1922 the Tour climbed the Col d'Izoard for the first time, and in 1924 Ottavio Bottecchia became the first Italian winner.

The race continued to develop. By 1928 it covered 24 stages, and in 1930 the trade teams were abolished and national teams introduced. A landmark occurred in 1937, when unnamed derailleur gears were permitted. Until then it had been the usual practice for competitors to turn their wheels around and use different sprockets for the mountains.

Before the Second World War the Tour staged its own battles between Italy's Gino Bartali and France's Roger Lapebe, with Lapebe winning in 1937 and Bartali in 1938. With the outbreak of war, the race was stopped and did not resume again until 1947.

Above left: *Adler advertising poster, 1920.*

Above right: *NSU advertising poster, 1925.*

Opposite: *Dunlop Cord advertising poster, 1925.*

LATER SAFETY BICYCLES: FROM WORLD
WAR TWO TO THE PRESENT DAY

The Second World War brought a limited return to the use of the bicycle in a military role. A special lightweight folding model for parachutists was developed for several armies, including the British. The British design of this machine had an elliptical tubular frame with a hinged top and bottom so that it could be folded in two by turning two wing nuts.

A period of stagnation followed the close of the Second World War. However, once this had passed, there was a revival in the general use of the bicycle and a parallel revival in the bicycle industry. The sale of new post-war bicycles benefited from a greater need for economy, while production was able to take advantage of the new precision machinery available. The industry expanded throughout the world, and soon bicycle touring, racing and travelling grew to become a fact of everyday life.

Wartime models had been of a standard design and uniformly black. The B.S.A. company advertisements counselled patience for the return of peace and, with it, of a full range of bicycles in bright colours. Raleigh encouraged people not to purchase a new bicycle but to keep their old model in good order and so leave the small numbers being produced for the war workers.

The cycling magazines of the period are filled with nostalgia for the good old days awheel in the countryside and the craftsmanship of bicycles gone by. P. Tonkin wrote, in the *Cyclists' Touring Club Gazette* of July 1942, about his memories of the golden age of the early 1900s and in particular the precision fittings and supreme quality of the "Sunbeam": "Bicycles built today are built to a simple design which lends itself most easily to mass production. Except for the trade mark one machine is much the same as another."

Correspondence also continued during the early 1940s on the subject of hub gears, brakes, dynamos and a host of additional problems. During the war Sturmey-Archer had suspended production but had not halted their research and development programme. One area of continued development was the hub dynamo, and this was a continual topic of contention for many cyclists. An A.D. Robertson wrote in the March 1941 edition of the *Cyclists' Touring Club Gazette*, regarding the dynamo: "the lack of light when stopped is rather a source of danger to the cyclists". His answer to this problem was, "I suppose one should also have a small stand-by battery to switch on when the dynamo is not generating".

*O*pposite: *Raleigh advertising poster from the 1950s.*

A bicyclist being runover by a tram in Amsterdam.

Shortly after the war such a unit was produced by Sturmey-Archer as an accessory to their dynohub. The Dry Accumulator Unit was a tubular container which was fixed to the seat tube and contained three two-volt RTV dry accumulator cells and a rectifier unit. The Dry Accumulator Unit provided a backup to the dynohub. If the cyclist using a dynohub came to a halt, the Dry Accumulator Unit automatically cut in to maintain illumination. However, this unit was short-lived; it had a tendency to leak.

Another interesting wartime development from Sturmey-Archer was patented in 1943. The practical effect of this patent was the introduction of the A.S.C. three-speed fixed hub, which was targeted at riders who preferred a fixed gear and who longed for a three-speed fixed.

Below: *Raleigh Little Winkie Tricycle, 1950s.*

Bottom: *Boy's B.S.A. 1953 cycle.*

World War II had forced the cancellation of the annual cycle show for ten years. When the show reopened at Earls Court, it was evident that Britain had been lagging behind the Continent in post-war progress. British touring machines of the late 1940s showed no deviation from the accepted lines, but rather had a tendency towards elaboration in minor details. The French and Italian models, in particular, were well designed and attractively finished. However, the opinion was that the British machines were better made – the premier machine at the 1949 show was the Dawes, which shone as the first for quality and finish – while the French machines were better designed. Some British machines showed Continental influences, such as the concealment of brake cables within frame tubes. This design was adopted in the Armstrong Cycles' machine, "The Super Continental".

Another obvious improvement seen at these early post-war shows was in the field of enamelling and plating. At this time visual appeal was important for many manufacturers and could be found in variegated finishes, chevrons, Continental linings of flamboyant lustres. However, this was not to everyone's taste. In an article in the 12 December 1951 edition of *The Bicycle*, John Crowe argued the point that, to release cycling from "semi-stagnation", cyclists should look to the small manufacturers who concentrated on attracting customers with advertisements for Continental accessories and "fancy finishes". To the small manufacturer he said: "it's up to you to improve the breed again".

Raleigh introduced the first up-to-date automatic process plant in the country and within five years production had increased by 150 per cent. Unable to cope with growing demand for exports, the company opened a ten-acre extension in 1952, and this was followed five years later by a further twenty-acre extension.

These cautious wartime and post-war years saw a considerable diversification in standard frame design, including the introduction of differing frame angles, a shorter

A bove: *Raleigh advertising poster, 1950.*

B elow: *A poster advertising the Italian film, 'Bicycle Thieves' (Ladri de biciclette), 1948.*

*R*aleigh advertising poster from 1950.

wheelbase, and stiffening of the rear triangle. The "Saxon" had twin seat tubes; the Paris "Galibier" a central strut lug; the "Bates" diadrant forks and cantiflex tubing; and a cradled bottom bracket appeared in the design of the elegant Thanet "Silverlight". The Thanet Company was first registered as a business in 1941 under the name "Thanet Cycles" by Les Cassell. Cassell was born in 1907 at Ramsgate in the Isle of

*T*he Telegram Boy.

Thanet, Kent. As a young man he had toured extensively on the Selbach machine. The bicycle he produced in these early years was called the "Silverthan" and had a top-class frame employing silver solder instead of brass to join the tubes. However, it was the "Silverlight" bicycle which made Thanet famous and gave the firm a worldwide reputation for finely crafted lightweight cycles. The year 1947 was the beginning of the "Silverlight" period. Promotional material claimed that the cradling of the bottom bracket was copied from the aircraft practice of cradling the engine. The approach of Cassell's extensive advertising campaign was just right for an austere post-war Britain, with its bright slogans, "Ease with Elegance" and "As Good as Gold and Brazed with Silver".

Silverlights and Silverthans were built mostly to be used as club machines or long-distance touring cycles. In 1952 the company had an order for a ladies Silverlight. The machine incorporated the bottom bracket arrangements and twin lateral tubes extending from the head lug to the rear drop out. The firm continued to be popular for a minority of connoissseurs, but unfortunately it petered to a close in 1968.

This was also an age of cycle components. In 1948 Sturmey-Archer had introduced an alloy shell weighing one-third as much as its steel counterparts. Stainless steel rims and parts were also introduced as British manufacturers competed with Italian and other foreign companies. Sturmey-Archer were clearly aware of such competition, although during the 1940s there was little development of rival gear systems. In 1944 Campag-

A PRODUCT OF RALEIGH INDUSTRIES

A Raleigh Cycle Company Advertisement for 'Robin Hood Cycles', 1950.

nolo had introduced the "Corsa" derailleur, and in 1950 this was developed into the Paris-Roubaix gear: however, the gear war soon recommenced. A correspondent at the 1955 Paris show said of Sturmey-Archer: "publicity is well conceived in its bold challenge to the derail systems of gearing".

Sturmey-Archer did not really recover at home until the 1950s. At the start of this decade they produced some fourteen hubs, six three-speed and five four-speed, and front hub brakes and front dynohubs. In 1954 they patented the Sturmey-Archer wide ratio six-speed, and later in the decade developed a new three-speed unit and flick switch devices.

The shows of the 1950s began to see a gradual narrowing of the gap between French and British design. Many firms in Britain were now, for example, assembling their frames without lugs and with concealed brake cables. However, by no means were all Continental ideas taken up in Britain, and many novelties were abandoned in the country of origin.

A typical French bicycle of this period made lavish use of chromium-plating, and employed mudguards of substantial quality and derailleur gears. Perfection was to be found in the specialist machines manufactured by Rene Herse and Alex Singer. These hand-made bicycles looked exceptional and cost a great deal. Even the large French manufacturers were still small compared with their British counterparts and thus enjoyed greater flexibility in the manufacturing process so that they could produce a variety of models which differed substantially from each other. By 1951 the British

manufacturers were producing 3½ million bicycles per year and exporting 2½ million to 140 countries.

Colour was still an important aspect of cycle sales. The 1955 Earls Court Show displayed such exciting shades that a fashion house might have been envious of them: Amaranthe, Amber Mist, Pearl Mist, Italian Red. Though some colours were subtle, others were more vulgar, mixing red with green, and electric shades of blue and red. Colour also spilled over into mudguards and accessories, to create an overall matching effect. Saddle firms, such as Midland, displayed tartan saddles as well as red, blue, maroon and green designs. On the Continent

Below: Delivering the evening edition.

*F*alxon B.M.X., 1985. The B.M.X. soon overtook the Chopper as the fashionable bicycle.

coloured tyres were popular, although they made little progress in Britain. Palmers, whose "Pixie" was produced in a white-walled version, were showing the same tyre with blue and green walls.

By the 1960 Earls Court Show, lightweight sports and cycle club models were making a noticeable comeback, having both been pushed into a corner by the 1958 show. Manufacturers, both large and small, had realized that cycling as a sport or pastime was by no means dead or dying.

In 1960, Raleigh Industries merged with TI (Tube Investments), thus gaining control of the Phillips, Hercules, Norman and Sun brands, to become the world's largest producers of two-wheeled transport.

The general trend during the early 1960s was to woo the teenager. Many show stands had models specifically designed to attract this generation. A colourful "off-the-peg" bicycle would be supplied with serious equipment, such as a Campagnolo ten-speed gear with centre-pull brakes, to give the teenager a good start in the game. Viking produced just such a model, and B.S.A. geared their advertising in a big way towards the youth market: "Dig that Hi-Fi Cycling It's Modern Man – it's B.S.A."

However, there were still cycles available for the "older generations and the connoisseur," among them the Carlton "Jewel" shown at the 1960 Earls Court Show. The Jewel cost £64 and represented true craftsmanship, fitted throughout with top-class

equipment, G.B. quick-release hubs, Ventoux bars, ten-speed Compag gears and a Unica saddle. Falcon too displayed a high-quality connoisseur cycle, the "San Remo", which was Campagnolo throughout and cost £73. The larger manufacturers showed well-equipped machines within a competitive price range. Raleigh offered the "Gran Sport" with G.B. centre-pull brakes and Compag gears. The five-speed model cost £27 19s 6d and the ten-speed £30 9s 6d. Phillips had a similar cycle range, including the "Black Shadow" with its cyclo super-60 ten-speed gear. This machine cost £25 19s 6d.

However, with the arrival of the 1960s cycling declined to a low ebb. New ideas were needed to turn the industry around and to create fresh interest. At the end of 1962 an innovative concept emerged to give the industry that boost. The machine in question was the result of Alex Moulton's experiments to see how a bicycle could be further improved.

Moulton had first produced a prototype of his small-wheeled bicycle in 1961 with 16-inch wheels and rubber suspension. He formed his own company and launched the Moulton Urban Bicycle in 1962. The new machine incorporated a single front suspension with nylon brushed steering splines, a rear suspension, 6¾-inch cranks and 16-inch wheels. The wheelbase was 44½ inches. This gave an open frame, which was easy to mount, so that the Moulton could be used as a general utility bicycle by all the family.

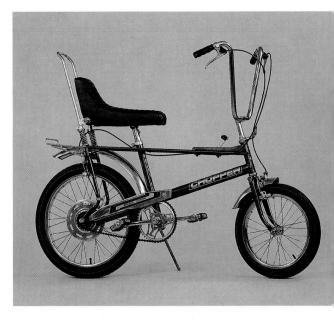

*R*ight: Raleigh Chopper. The Chopper was the first of the action bicycles that have become so popular over the last twenty years.

In 1964 the *Cyclists' Touring Club Gazette* reviewed the machine: "The Moulton is . . . the first serious attempt since the Recumbent Cycle at introducing a new approach to cycle design." In May of that year the Moulton achieved the Design Centre Award. The judges commented that it was "a radical re-thinking of conventional bicycle design, excellently engineered for ease and comfort". However, it also provoked criticism, that it was just a rethinking of an old and tired theme, with the rider sill occupying the same position on the machine, the front wheel still being steered by handlebars, the cycle still being propelled by rotating cranks through chain-drive to the rear wheel, and that spring suspension was not a new concept at all. Many of these comments came from "serious cyclists" whose first and last love would always be the diamond-frame Safety bicycle.

In 1965 Raleigh introduced their own small-wheel bicycle the "RSW16", and a folding version called the "Compact". The "RSW14", a smaller-wheel model for children, was launched in 1966 and in 1968 a 20-inch wheel model appeared.

The early 1970s were highly profitable years for the cycle industry in general, although British-made hub gears were facing a hard time as the popularity of the derailleur system grew and there was an influx of foreign products. Sturmey-Archer were involved in many intensive developments, including a new coaster brake and a new three-speed with a no-slip position between the gears. In 1973 a seven-speed hub was patented, but this unit was not produced.

Another breakthrough in traditional bicycle design occurred in 1970. Launched in 1969 in the United States, the "Chopper" was the first of the action bicycles that have been developed over the last twenty years or so. In ten years it sold 750,000 models. In 1970, the Chopper was advertised in Britain along the lines of a motorcycle or sports car for children too young to have either. These children could experience the same excitement at a tender age through this ungainly machine, with its high handlebars and banana seat.

However, the Chopper soon disappeared to be replaced by a new fashion-setter, the B.M.X. The raw beginnings of the Bicycle Motor Cross were established in 1969 in America, with legitimate racing organized in the 1970s. It started with children gathering in fields to ride in imitation of motorcycle-riders. The bicycle popular among these enthusiasts was called a "Stingray" (a Schwinn Bicycle Company trade mark). These machines were modified for racing by their riders to bring about a weight reduction and increased strength. It became apparent that a special bicycle was needed, and towards the close of 1975 companies began to make B.M.X. bikes, and to sponsor and

A B.M.X. 'Pogo' Freestyle competition. Photograph by Richard Francis.

put together racing teams. The most popular bike to hit the market was the "Mongoose", which appeared in 1976.

In 1976 Raleigh launched the "Grifter", a "safe" version of the American B.M.X. bicycle. With no specially designed B.M.X. machine in Britain children began to remove mudguards from conventional cycles and race them across obstacles and rough ground. Although the Grifter pointed the way ahead, it was not until 1982 that Raleigh launched the B.M.X. "Burner" range.

Professional racing began in America in 1977 and in 1979 the craze had reached Australia. By 1980 racing was big business in Britain as well, with tracks, championships, sponsorship programmes and promotion coming a top priority among many manufacturers.

The B.M.X. may be ideal for off-the-road use and for performing stunts, but it is no substitute for a conventional bicycle, being too low-geared and too heavy for regular road use. During the last twenty years the more conventional machines have covered the whole spectrum of design, from traditional to purpose-built aerodynamic models tailored solely for speed. An example of this diversity was seen at the 1978 International Cycle Show where one of the more popular models on show was the Pashley "Princess". The Princess was an elegant all-black loop frame, with 28-inch wheels, basket, full chainguard, stirrup brakes and a three-speed hub gear, all for £94. Pashley stated that they had a great demand for their

Princess, especially from France.

The 1990s could prove to be the decade of the mountain bike. Mountain biking is now a permanent and established branch of cycling. In 1989 just under 900,000 mountain bikes were sold, most of which were purchased by adults. Ideal for commuting and off-road competitions alike, the mountain bike is constantly being improved, although its basic design has remained the same, with straight bars, handlebar mounted gears, cantilever brakes and 26-inch wheels. The strength of the joints has been improved with aluminium tubing, incorporating forged steel lugs and bottom bracket shell.

Top: *Raleigh Low Profile, c. 1984.*

Middle: *Kirk Precision, 1989.*

Opposite: *Mountain bikes.*

Left: *Moulton Touring Bicycle, 1973.*

RACING

After World War II racing took on a new lease of life. Great advances in track bicycle design produced machines of ultra-lightweight steel frames and alloy components, allowing previously unheard-of records. Over the years there were many superb winners, many memorable incidents and many heroes and heroines.

In 1947 the Tour de France resumed after the war and was won by Frenchman Jean Robic. Bartali rode again in 1949 against one of the world's greatest riders, the Italian Fausto Coppi, who also had a reputation for being a playboy and scandalized his country by parading his mistress, although he was soon dubbed "Il Campionissimo" (Champion of Champions).

Coppi was born in 1919, in Costellania, Italy, and died following an illness in 1960. Between 1938 and 1957, he boasted 130 major victories, including the world road championship in 1953 and the world pursuit championship in 1947 and 1949. Coppi became Italian road champion in 1942, 1947, 1949 and 1955, and national pursuit champion in 1940, 1941, 1942, 1947 and 1948. In 1942 he set up the world one-hour record on track and covered 45 kilometres 798 metres. There were great battles between Bartali and Coppi throughout the Tour de France, which Coppi won in 1949 and 1952. In 1940 he won his first Giro of Italy, a success he repeated in 1947, 1949, 1952 and 1953. Included in the list of his prestigious achievements are the Grand Prix des Nations won in 1946 and 1947, and the Milan–San Remo, won in 1946, 1948 and 1949.

The 1940s and early 1950s were fruitful and exciting years for racing and produced heroes and heroines who are still talked about today. One such cyclist rode for the Manchester Wheelers and his name dominated cycle sport throughout this period. As early as 1939 Reg Harris had been selected for the world amateur sprint championships and in 1947 he won the world amateur sprint track championship, the first of his five world titles, and, incidentally, the first world title for a Briton since Bill Bailey's victory in 1913.

At the 1948 Olympics Harris achieved two silvers, in the 1,000-metres sprint and the 2,000-metres tandem with A. Bannister. Harris signed with Raleigh as a professional in 1949 and that same year he won the world's record for 1,000 metres and a further six national records. In both 1950 and 1954 he won the world championships. Even after leaving the sport Reg Harris could not be prevented from securing victories. In 1974 he came out of retirement at the age of 54 and took out his 25-year-old cycle to win again.

Next to the great Reg Harris, the most successful pure sprinter that Britain has produced in post-war years was probably Cyril Peacock, who in 1954 won the world

Below: *Bartali winner of the Tour de France, 1948, parades at the Parc de Prince terminal of the 25 day race around France.*

The Italian Fausto Coppi. One of the world's greatest riders, Coppi won 130 major victories between 1938 and 1957.

amateur sprint championship – the same year that Harris won the professional title.

In 1950 Ferdi Kubler was the first Swiss rider to win the Tour de France, and the climbs of Puy de Dome and the fateful Ventoux were added to the course. In 1953 the green jersey for points winner was introduced. It was not until 1958 that the first Englishman, Brian Robinson, won a stage of the Tour, an achievement he repeated the following year.

Britain also can boast its classic event – The Milk Race – whose beginnings are rooted in these post-war years of true grit and heroic achievements. The forerunner of the Milk Race began in 1951, the first winner of this Tour de la Grande-Bretagne was Ian Steel, who in the following year won the Peace Race through the German Democratic Republic, Poland and Czechoslovakia.

The Tour of Britain had initially come into being because the British League of Cyclists and the National Cycle Union needed a stage race. The only large event of this kind was the Brighton to Glasgow race, which lasted six days. The *Daily Express* sponsored the race from 1954 to 1956, then the National Dairy Council agreed to back

it. The first winner of the newly named Milk Race was the Austrian Richard Durlacher, in 59 hours, 53 minutes and 59 seconds. The prize money was £1,250. In 1959 the first Briton took the race, and Bill Bradley went on to win in 1960 as well.

The Milk Race developed into an inter-

Harris, 1949. Harris won five world titles.

Above: *Eric van Lancker of Belgium, 1984. Photograph by Mike Hewitt.*

Previous Page: *The Milk Race, 1984. The Milk Race is so called because it is backed by the National Dairy Council. Photograph by Richard Francis.*

national event in 1962 with Poland, the Scandinavian countries and Czechoslovakia competing. Poland won the race for the first time in 1966, and again in 1978 with Jan Brzezny. The year 1966 saw the first Russian competitor, although it was not until 1977 that a Russian won the race. In 1974 the race was ridden over its shortest distance, at 922 miles (1,475 kilometres), while in 1986 the race held was some 1,650 miles. The first American to win was Matt Eaton in 1983, and in 1984 Oleg Czougeda became the sixth Russian to win the Milk Race in eight years. The first professional trade teams competed in 1985, with Raleigh-Weinmann and Fangio (Belgium) taking part. The first professional winner was the Belgian rider Eric Van Lancker. The following year saw the first British winner for ten years, Joey McLoughlin of the A.N.C. Halfords team. This team also produced the 1987 winner, Malcolm Elliott. Russia won again in 1988, with Vasily Zhdanov. The first Canadian, Brian Walton (7-Eleven Team), won in 1989, and 1990 saw the first victory for an Australian, Shane Sutton (Banana-Falcon).

The internationally recognized governing body for road and track racing in Britain was formed in 1959. This organization emerged from a bitter struggle between the N.C.U. and the B.L.R.C. and they joined to form the British Cycling Federation.

Originally founded in 1878 as the Bicycle Union, the N.C.U. had taught the world the racing game. As far back as 1876 the general feeling in the cycling world was that some form of legislative body was needed to govern the sport, a view which was supported in both the cycling and sporting press of the period.

In November 1877, The London, Pickwick, Surrey and Temple Bicycle Clubs jointly agreed to establish the Bicycle Union. A lengthy prospectus was circulated to all the clubs in Britain, with an invitation to attend the first general meeting in February 1878. In brief the prospectus stated that the Union's aims were:

1. To secure justice for the cyclist and to safeguard his rights on the road.
2. To watch legislative moves in Parliament and elsewhere affecting the cyclist, and to make representations when necessary.
3. To improve the relations of cyclists with the railways; to cut the cost of transporting a bicycle by rail; and to improve methods of conveyance.
4. To frame definitions, recommend rules for racing, and to arrange for amateur championships.

Right: *Robinson in the Tour de France, 1960.*

From an initial attendance by 24 club delegates, developments and events moved swiftly. The first national track championships were held at Stamford Bridge on 11 May 1878, with two agreed distances of 2 miles and 25 miles. The following year the championships were revised and extended to include events over 1, 5, 25 and 50 miles, all of which were won in that year by H. L. Cortis of the Wanderers C.C. Shortly afterwards tricycle championships were also instituted.

1879 was a historic year for another reason: the debate over "amateur" question. The Bicycle Union issued a definition of an amateur, or rather it defined a professional and said that anyone who did not fall within that definition was an amateur. On this point and many others the union aroused a deal of heated discussion, and received a flood of threats and protests from various athletic organizations and individuals. The French, particularly the Parisians, said that the definition was too hard on the amateur: he should be allowed 2,000 francs for expenses each time he rode!

The first five or six meetings of the B.U. were not remarkable productive. In addition to the planning of the championships, it published a set of twelve recommendations on riding a bicycle on the road, one of which contained instructions on what to do when meeting and overtaking a horse. Then, in 1883 the B.U. changed its name to the National Cyclists' Union.

Between 1883 and 1885 under the direction of its president, the Earl of Albemarle, the new N.C.U. was energetic in supporting the cause of cyclists and cycling, with particular emphasis on the improvement of road conditions. It is also noteworthy for having been the first sporting organization to set a standard for timekeeping and timekeepers.

Alongside the progressive measures there were setbacks also, including arguments with the Amateur Athletic Association (founded in 1880) and massive reorganization in the 1930s. In 1942 a further problem arose with the advent of open road racing. The N.C.U. was involved in a bitter struggle with the British League of Racing Cyclists (founded in 1942). This acrimonious dispute was to remain a blot on British cycling until 1 February 1959 when peace was restored as the N.C.U. and B.L.R.C. merged their separate identities into the British Cycling Federation. The B.C.F. is still the national body for road and track racing and also supports time trials.

The 1950s continued to be eventful years, with Ken Joy, the holder of the 100-mile and 12-hour competition records, securing the title of British best all-rounder between 1949 and 1952. Joy eventually signed as a professional in 1953 with the Hercules Cycle and Motor Company Limited.

In 1952 another Briton claimed fame. Ken Russell had been steadily improving his performances since 1946 until they culminated in a win of the 1952 Tour of Britain on an Ellis Briggs machine. The late 1940s and early 1950s were also eventful times for *Beryl Burton.*

Opposite left: *Merckx in the victory wreath of flowers of Het Volk. Eddy Merckx dominated international cycling in the 1970s and he won the Tour de France five times for Belgium: 1969, 1970–72 and 1974.*

Opposite right: *Looking for a four-leaf clover . . . for luck. Britain's Tommy Simpson is seen on his hands and knees before the start of the 2nd lap of the Tour de France. 4th July 1967.*

women cyclists. In 1947 Stella Farrell brought the W.R.R.A. 25-mile record down from 1 hour, 9 minutes, 29 seconds to 1 hour, 5 minutes, 31 seconds, a time subsequently reduced by Joyce Dean to 1 hour, 3 minutes and 29 seconds. Stella Farrell also completed the Brighton-and-back in a new time of 5 hours, 6 minutes, 35 seconds.

The number of record rides increased throughout this period, and championships were won and competition records broken by numerous talented women, including

Susie Denham (née Rimmington), Stella Farrell, Joyce Harris (née Dean), Elsie Harton, Joyce Brooker, Daisy Stockwell and Eileen Sheridan, the most outstanding lady road cyclist of the post-war era. Eileen Sheridan rode for the Coventry C.C. and won three championships and five record performances on the road in 1950 on a Hercules bicycle. She was the best all-rounder of 1949 and 1950 and the holder of the women's competition records at 30, 50 and 100 miles, and over twelve hours. In addition to this

Right: *Zoop Zoetemelk for Holland.*

Sean Kelly for Ireland in the Tour de France, 1989. Photograph by Mark Wohlwender.

she also held the W.R.R.A. record for the routes from Birmingham to London and London to Oxford and back and was national champion at 50 and 100 miles.

Towards the close of the 1950s there emerged another outstanding figure in women's racing. In 1959 Beryl Burton (Leeds) won the first of the seven world championships she was to attain between 1959 and 1967.

The 1960s also had their fair share of triumphs. Eddy Merckx laid claim to being the best cyclist ever when he made his Tour de France debut to win in 1969, for he had already won several world titles. Merckx won four more Tours and nearly all the one-day classics as well, not once but several times, before he retired in 1975. However, the 1960s will be best remembered for one man and his overwhelming desire to prove that a Briton could beat the world in the Tour de France: an obsession which possibly caused his untimely death 6,720 feet above the Rhône Valley on Mont Ventoux.

Tom Simpson was born in Durham in 1937. The family then moved to Harworth, Nottinghamshire, where he joined the Harworth & District C.C., and he made his racing debut at the tender age of 13. In these early years he earned the nickname "The

Four Stone Coppi" for his spirit and determination. Simpson was still a novice when he entered the 1956 national championship held at the Fallowfield Track in Manchester and came second. The same year he was dubbed "The Sparrow" during his racing tours of Russia and Bulgaria and he won a bronze medal for the British Olympic quartet pursuit team in Australia, with Dan Burgess, John Geddes and Mike Gambrill.

In 1957 Simpson won nearly every 25-mile road time trial in which he competed, and also the B.L.R.C. national amateur hill-climb championship. He rode again for Britain in 1958, in Bulgaria, and in 1959, at the age of 21, Simpson left Britain and eventually became domiciled in Belgium and France. During his first season in Brittany he applied for an independent (semi-professional) licence and raced in local events in the colours of the Velo Club, Briochin. He was then offered a place in the St. Rapha-Velo Club 12e Team to race in the Route de

France, a tough eight-stage race for riders aged under 25. Simpson won the final stage.

In the Rapha squad for the eight-day Tour de L'Ouest, Simpson won the fifth day stage and race leadership. On the sixth day he won the time trial stage, only to lose it all on the following day.

Simpson now achieved his full professional licence. During the world professional pursuit championships held in Amsterdam, he was knocked out in the quarter finals, but before the close of the 1959 season Simpson had raced against the great Coppi and claimed a total of 28 victories.

Then came his debut in the Tour de France as a member of the British team, along with John Kennedy, Stan Brittain, Norman Sheil, Jock Andrews, Vic Sutton, Harry Reynolds and Brian Robinson. Simpson began well, although unfortunately his strength declined until he reached Paris in twenty-ninth position overall. His first victory in Road Classics came in the 1961

Above: Mike Kloser of the U.S.A., World Champion competing in the Grundig World Cup in London. Photograph by Mike Hewitt.

Opposite: Greg Lemond in the Tour de France, 1990. Lemond has won the Tour de France three times: 1986, 1989 and 1990. Two years before he rode to victory for the second time he was nearly killed in a shooting accident. Photograph by Graham Watson.

Greg Lemond wearing the yellow jersey in the Tour de France, 1990. Photograph by Graham Watson.

140-mile Tour of Flanders.

The year 1962 saw Simpson become the first Briton to take the coveted yellow jersey of overall leadership in the Tour de France. Although he lost the jersey next day, he held sixth place when the race ended in Paris. One of his specialities became the two-man relay race. In Madrid, during the six-day track racing, he finished third with the Australian Johnny Tresider.

At the start of 1963 Simpson switched to the Peugeot-B.P. squad, with whom he remained until the end. With the Peugeot squad he won the Grand Prix Parisienne team time trial, and in Super Prestige Pernod Points competition he came second to the great Jacques Anquetil.

In 1965 he became the number one world professional road race champion. The year 1967 saw Simpson in high spirits. He had stage wins in the Tour of Sardinia and the Tour of Spain. The Tour de France in 1967 reverted to the practice of accepting entries from national rather than trade teams and the British team were riding well. Simpson was burning with ambition and determined to win. Although he had first established his base in the Breton town of St Brieuc, later moving to Paris and finally settling in Ghent, he managed both to become a Fleming and to retain his national, British, pride.

His greatest dream was to see Britain rule in the world of cycling. This ambition and his great will to win finally pushed him to the limit and on 13 July 1967, during Stage 13 in the 54th Tour de France, Tom Simpson died. The Ventoux claimed the 29-year-old cyclist in a sweltering 130 degree heat, 6,720 feet above the Rhône Valley.

The 1980s saw a profusion of great talents. In 1980 Britain's Tony Doyle won the world professional pursuit in France, only weeks after turning professional. Bernard Hinault, of France, joined Jacques Anquetil (France) and Eddy Merckx (Belgium) in 1985 as a five-times winner of the Tour de France. In 1986 Greg Lemond of America won the Tour, and went on to repeat his performance in 1989 and 1990. In 1988, Sean Yates won a Tour stage, the first Englishman to do so since 1975.

July 1984 saw the first Tour de France Féminin, which was won by the American Marianne Martin, with the Briton Clare Greenwood seventh. The great British female riders from this period include Vicky Thomas, Maria Blower and Sally Hodge.

The outstanding Italian rider Maria Canins won in 1985 and 1986. Canins had begun cycling at the age of 32 after being a top-class cross-country skier with twelve national titles to her name. Her chief rival was Jeannie Longo of France who finished second to Canins in 1985 and 1986. In 1988 and 1989 Longo's revenge was sweet when Canins came second to Longo's first. Longo had also begun her sporting career as a skier in the slalom and started cycling in 1979. She won the world championships over Canins in 1985.

Women's racing in the 1990s presents a frustrating picture. Women still earn less than men and, to date, there are only 170 women licence-holders in Britain. The largest women's cycle race in Britain is the Women's Racing Association's three-day stage race in May, for which teams enter from all over Western Europe. The Tour de France Féminin ceased in 1989: another nail in the coffin for women's cycle sport since fewer races means fewer novices to keep the sport alive. It is also a sad fact that in these days of equality there are no professional women cyclists.

CONCLUSION:
MODERN DESIGNS AND BEYOND

Does the past hold the answers to the future? The previous chapters have shown only a glimpse into the bizarre, colourful, oft-times contentious and yet always fascinating history of the cycle. The story goes on, and as developments continue there is a new emphasis on and a new appreciation of the past. The most important question to be asked when considering modern and future designs is this: can the diamond frame ever be improved upon? Rather than experimenting with various design changes, will manufacturers attempt to perfect the diamond frame by finding new solutions to problems of overall efficiency and responsiveness?

The question of responsiveness in relation to the diamond-frame design is not new. In the mid-1930s manufacturers were attracted by ultra-short wheelbases, and the more satisfactory of their designs included the Baines VS37 and 38 "Flying Gate". This model incorporated a displaced seat tube, which rose vertically from the bottom bracket shell to make a T-junction with the top tube. A seat pin was supported in a short separate tube, the lower end of which was braced by a second pair of ultra-slim seat stays joining the T-junction to the rear ends.

A different approach to the design question could be seen in Horace Bates' cantiflex tube design of the 1950s, incorporating diadrant forks with compensating curves; the Dunelt fork (diadrant in reverse); the Granby taper tube; and the Hetchins design which deployed the use of curly stays. The Hetchins were machines for connoisseurs and were designed in such a way as to abandon rigidity in the interests of comfort. At the 1954 Earls Court Show, a *CTC*

Gazette correspondent remarked: "Fancy lugwork may not make the machine run any easier, but it certainly increases pride of ownership."

The search for the ideal cycle design may look to the past, and it may also be in vain. In truth, it may be never-ending and cover all aspects of cycle design, such as lightness, ideal angles and materials. These aspects, in turn, will differ when related to the four main types of cycles produced: racers, tourers, utility and children's models.

Could the so-called "Space-age" materials be the way forward: titanium, magnesium, carbon fibre, plastics? Manufacturers have, in fact, already been along this road. In 1945 L.A. Sansam wrote in the August edition of the *CTC Gazette* that he wished a really modern bicycle in the near future could be made from magnesium alloy. At the 1954 Earls Court Show Hercules exhibited an experimental machine with frame tubes

Opposite: Cycle courier. Photograph by Chris Barry.

Francesco Moser for Italy in the National Track Championships in Leicester, August 1987. Moser won several of the classic races and made two world track records. Photograph by Richard Francis.

made from glass fibre. Their claim was that this tube was five times lighter than its equivalent in steel yet just as strong. The correspondent wrote in awe of this "Tantalising glimpse of future".

The only advance will come when scientists discover a new form of material which is lighter, stronger and more flexible than any previously available. If such a material is ever found it is certain to be adopted by the professional racing teams.

The racing machine of the future may well display a completely different design from that of the touring cycle. Made from exotic materials, it could be streamlined with regard to aerodynamics. One example already seen is the machine used by Bernard Hinault and his Renault team-mates for the time trials in the 1979 Tour de France. The "Gitane" employed elongated rims and oval tubing; it also used a Fairings disc wheel and many other advanced component parts, such as gearing, just to get that one second ahead of any other competitor.

There will always be controversy over bicycle design and new technology, especially when it comes to racing and record attempts. However, it is difficult to say whether there should be stricter rules regulating basic frame design, tubing sizes, materials and wheel dimensions, or whether the authorities will adopt a no-holds-barred attitude and dispense with any restricting regulations. We might consider these points when looking at the design of the cycle Francesco Moser used for his 1988 world indoor one-hour record. This machine caused great consternation among the Unione Cycling Inernationale Technical Commission, who cast doubt on the record because the "bicycle shown was not of a 'normal type' " and therefore, "cannot be accepted by the Technical Commission of the UCI for setting new records". Moser's cycle was basically of a traditional design, but had a divided seat tube, disc wheels and a rear wheel of 105 centimetres in diameter.

Many well-trodden avenues are likely to be re-explored in the future, particularly in the areas of streamlining, aerodynamics, lightness and weatherproofing. The question of weatherproofing could be expanded to include durability, a principal factor in the production of children's cycles. One ideal material for children's cycles would be plastic, which is already successfully deployed in modern cycles for parts of derailleur gears, wheels and rims. Plastic saves weight, does not corrode and is durable. However, the first bicycle to be produced with frame, forks, wheels and handlebars all injection-moulded in plastic was a commercial failure. The Itera Cyklen was manufactured in Sweden, in 1982. Although it was light, strong and would not rust, the Itera Cyklen had one unredeemable feature – it was ugly!

Apart from wanting an up-to-the-minute cycle with additional designer accessories, children will require matching, colour-coordinated graphics on their helmets, knee and elbow pads, boots and even cycle suits. The new 1991 Moulton, the "AM" had 17-inch tyres, suspension and a collection of such specially designed accessories from zipper fairings and aerodisc wheels, to carriers, bags and child seats.

In future years the increased awareness of environmental concerns may well encourage more people to leave their cars in the garage, and the utility cycle may thus gain increased popularity among the shopper and commuter alike. A popular breed of utility model is the folding cycle. One such design was the

Cyclo Cross, 1986. Photograph by Richard Francis.

B.M.X. stunt riding. Photograph by Richard Francis.

Bickerton, whose box frame was made entirely from aluminium and was hinged in the centre with a special clamp for easy storage. A recent British design in small-wheel folding cycles was the 1988 "Strida", which can be folded like a baby's buggy. The strength of the frame relies on the principles of a triangle and the drum brakes provide efficient stopping power.

Other types of utility cycle do not fold. In 1991 Pashley are producing purpose-built cycles for city streets, described by the manufacturers as "equipped to the right specification for the job in hand".

Another area of possible future experimentation lies in frame building. Does a frame have to be made from tubes and lugs? One solution may be found in the stamped

frame, an example of which is the 1989 Kirk Precision machine, whose magnesium frame of computer-aided design aims to provide the most energy-efficient and rigid version possible. Magnesium was used because it is the lightest structured metal and such a frame can be stronger and stiffer than a conventional frame of equivalent weight. Magnesium is also abundant: a cubic metre of sea-water contains enough to make one frame. This is pressure die-cast in a steel mould, and steel inserts are subsequently bonded in place to take the headset, bottom bracket, seat post and various other attachment points.

Finally there is the future of the tourer to consider. Will new models look much as they do today, with the whole sophisticated frame design and the component parts geared towards the racing machines, or will they claim a deal of sophisticated technology for themselves? In point of fact, touring cycles have a long life span, which means that in the year 2010 many touring cyclists could still be riding their 1991 models.

Since around 1910 the bicycle's efficiency has been enhanced in many ways, by reducing weight, altering the position of the rider, and improving tyres and other accessories, including gearing systems. Indeed, it may be through gearing systems that the tourer finally achieves its full potential by means of automatic gearing which continually changes in accordance with the terrain.

The future touring machine may favour the recumbent rather than the conventional style of bicycle. Looking more like a two-wheeled motor car, it could be made from light aluminium alloy with fairings and front-wheel drive. Recumbents are comfortable for long-distance cycling: the rider sits with bottom and back totally supported. However, in heavy traffic they are not so easy to manoeuvre as a conventional cycle.

The recumbent design is not a new concept, having been developed before World War I. In 1913 Etienne Buneau invented a torpedo cycle, and Varilla and Marcel Riffard bent wooden spurs covered with smooth material over an upright bicycle. The machine weighed 17 kilogrammes and with it Marcel Berthet took the one-kilometre record from 50.9 to 57.3 kilometres per hour. Riffard and Berthet then created a bicycle

Opposite: B.M.X. racing – general view of hoops. Photograph by Richard Francis.

Snow biking in the Swiss Alps. Photograph by Mark Wohlwender.

made from aluminium with spruce and tulip magnolia fairings covered in varnished linen. Called "Velodyne 1", it weighed only 14 kilogrammes.

In 1933 Berthet set a new world one-hour record of 48.6 kilometres in Paris, and two months later he increased this to 49.992. The same year saw Francis Faure take the hour record for an unfaired recumbent to 45.056 kilometres. In 1934, the International Cycling Federation redefined standard bicycle dimensions to exclude recumbents.

George Mochet and Francis Faure attacked the one-hour record in a fully enclosed model with a varnished body. The distance was raised to 50.537 kilometres.

Development of the recumbent then slackened until the 1970s, when a fresh interest evolved in the United States. The International Human Powered Vehicle Association encouraged both bicycle and tricycle recumbents, with lightweight fairings, to break new records, mostly on machines made by individuals.

The 1980s saw a short-lived revival in recumbent design – the Sinclair C5. Not strictly a cycle as though it could be pedalled it was mostly powered by rechargeable electrical batteries, the C5 was described as a new concept in personal transport. It provided an intimate vehicle which was environmentally friendly and cost-effective.

However, it failed because although basically a good idea, its low position caused people to feel vulnerable, especially when competing for road space with a juggernaut!

The technology and aesthetics of bicycle engineering will certainly continue to improve and may be dictated by the higher quality and precision of new instruments and design mechanisms. As more and more adults return to the bicycle, the future looks secure. Many people have developed an interest in health and fitness, and to achieve the "body beautiful" they have taken to cycling in a big way. A practical, open-air pastime, cycling actually burns away more calories than jogging or swimming.

Environmental issues are also bringing forth a new generation of cyclists and manufacturers are quick to encourage them. The cycle is a true friend of the earth. With motor vehicles congesting and polluting the towns and cities, many commuters are donning their face-masks and risking the onslaught. The evolution of future cycle designs may be gradual, reflecting both public taste and the continuous pursuit of lightness and efficiency, but heralding a new "Golden Age" in which touring will thrive. We shall perhaps see a mass exodus from the concrete jungle and its polluted atmosphere as cyclists rip off their face-masks and breathe in the sweet air.

COLLECTING

There are many kinds of collectors. At one end of the scale are those who collect for themselves, hoarding artefacts in their private shrines and at the other end are the museums and galleries, open to the public to educate and entertain while collecting and preserving artefacts for future generations.

Certainly so long as there are things to collect there will be collectors, the scarcer the collectable objects becoming the more avid the collector and the higher price he is prepared to pay, whether his field be bird eggs or butterflies, Rembrandts or Rodins, motor cars, motorcycles or cycles. The prices at auctions vary from millions of pounds for some paintings, hundreds of thousands for cars, and tens of thousands for motorcycles. In this book we are interested only in the collection of cycles, some models fetching many thousands of pounds at auctions, and associated items.

There are many different motives for collecting them. Some have a genuine affection for these machines, having acquired a cycle they lovingly restore it, ride it occasionally and show it off to like minded enthusiasts. The pre-pneumatic era is the most highly prized, although any cycle made before 1914 will always be snapped up. As these are getting scarcer and harder to obtain, some collectors are turning to the specialist hand-built lightweight cycle of the 1930s.

There are those who collect a particular make, already having a car and a motorcycle of the same marque, such as the Sunbeam, Raleigh, B.S.A., Lea Francis, etc., and love to show off their complete set. Again there are those who amass a huge number, not to show or ride but to hoard in sheds and garages, very often in a poor state of renovation and restoration, but the pleasure comes from the actual owning of more and more – and more. Then there are others who collect as an investment, the machines being acquired in the hope that their value will increase but having no more interest or sentimental value than stocks and shares.

There are owners of moderately large collections who with great care refurbish and restore their machines and put them on show to the public. Although not strictly museums as they have no guarantee of continuity and their main aim is the pleasure and satisfaction of the owner above that of the public, they perform a useful and sometimes valuable service in preserving the machines and bringing something of history to those who pay to view.

Cycles themselves are not the only desirables. There is a great call for the many artefacts, beautiful and as rare as the machines they complement, from not only the collectors of cycles but also those who have insufficient space or indeed money to aim for the actual machines themselves.

Lamps are popular collectors items whether they are candle, oil or acetylene. Decorative and elegant they are a joy to behold when renovated and polished so the chrome, nickel, copper or brass sparkles. Together with the lamps are the tins and canisters which held the oil or carbide without which the lamps could not function, often beautifully decorated and flamboyantly coloured.

Warning devices, mostly bells of all shapes and sizes, tones and beauty, together with hooters, cyclist's way-clearer whistles and sirens are also sought after. Then there are brightly patterned dress cords which were woven into intricate patterns, oil cans, tool bags, rare gears and pumps. The list of items is as large as the list of artefacts.

The original issues of early cycling books, such as *Bartleets Bicycle Book*, G. Lacy Hillier's book *Cycling* from the Badminton Library of Sports and Pastimes, John Sowerby's *I Got on my Bicycle*, *Fifty Years a Cyclist* by A.W. Rumney, the original issue of *Canterbury Pilgrimage*, old time cycling manuals, C.T.C. and N.C.U. touring handbooks, race meeting programmes etc, etc.. The list is almost endless.

Enamel advertising signs for cycles are much sought after. Also posters, which when framed could adorn any room, postcards, prints and photographs, all with the cycle motif, later copies as well as originals, they all depict so beautifully eras from the past years of cycling.

Collecting is an absorbing interest in itself and the acquisition of rare objects of esca-lating value adds even more to the hobby.

Public owned museums or a museum which is a Charitable Trust are probably the most important collectors from the public's point of view as their collections are cared for and put on show to the public. The most important of these in England, the National Cycle Museum at Lincoln, is unable to benefit from the rising values as being a Charitable Trust it is unable to dispose of anything at all in its collection. Indeed the rising prices and values are a disadvantage as they make it very difficult to buy many objects it would dearly like to put on display to the public.

So, collect for interest's sake, do not hoard for the sake of hoarding, remember always that there are others who are equally interested, and enjoy every aspect of the useful and delightful invention of the cycle, riding, racing, touring, collecting, reading and socializing. Without the cycle the world would be a poorer place.

Index

Page numbers in *italic* refer to the illustrations

INDEX